You're Invited Backstage . . . .

Perhaps the best regular stunt feature I developed for the show involved one of the nicest ladies ever to appear on it—Joan Embry, an animal handler at the San Diego Zoo. I can remember the first time she was on: one of the animals she brought with her was a young elephant named Carol that she had taught to paint. This elephant picked up a brush with her trunk, dipped it into a bucket of paint and then "created" a mural on the floor. Of course, she got paint all over Johnny. It was a hysterical spot and turned out to be the first of many, since I made the joyous discovery that the only time Johnny didn't mind being upstaged was when he was being upstaged by an animal.

Johnny always liked to see Joan bring elephants on the show—not only because he rather liked them, but because he had learned very early on that if he put a handful of peanuts in his pants pockets, the elephant would smell them and keep going for Johnny's crotch with its trunk.

CRAIG TENNIS

JOHNNY TONIGHT!

PUBLISHED BY POCKET BOOKS NEW YORK

Distributed in Canada by PaperJacks Ltd., a Licensee
of the trademarks of Simon & Schuster, a division of
Gulf + Western Corporation.

Another *Original* publication of POCKET BOOKS

POCKET BOOKS, a Simon & Schuster division of
GULF & WESTERN CORPORATION
1230 Avenue of the Americas, New York, N.Y. 10020
In Canada distributed by PaperJacks Ltd.,
330 Steelcase Road, Markham, Ontario.

ISBN: 0-671-41451-8

First Pocket Books printing September, 1980

10 9 8 7 6 5 4 3 2 1

POCKET and colophon are trademarks of Simon & Schuster.

Interior design by Sofia Grunfeld

Printed in Canada

Preface

Craig Tennis worked for Johnny Carson for eight years and two days. By the time he left "The Tonight Show" to become a television producer in his own right, Craig had for several years filled the key position of head talent coordinator for Johnny, responsible for the selection, screening, and booking of many of the guests on the show.

On Craig's last evening on the job, Johnny surprised him—*and* the staff. He interrupted the show to bid Craig a personal farewell. It went like this. . . .

"For the past eight years, Craig Tennis has been with this show," said Johnny, "and for the last few of those years, he's been serving as our head talent coordinator. Now he's leaving us to go on and do other things."

Johnny paused, fidgeting with his pencils. "This is a tough show to do. It's tough for the people who have to line up the guests—and it's especially tough," he deadpanned, "for the people who have to talk with Craig. . . ."

"Oh yes"—smiled Johnny, warming to the laughter—
"Craig is also the one who has been responsible for
most of those stunts which have threatened to take
my life. Like jumping off a 20-foot platform, breath-
ing fire, putting my head through a board—what was
the latest one, Craig? Of course—he wanted me to
swim Hell Gate. He thought that would *really* be fun."
More laughter.

"Yes, friends, all these wonderful things . . . but—"
Johnny looked down at his hands and said, "Craig has
done an absolutely super job with this show. He has
contributed so much to it that I really, really hate to
lose him." More fidgeting. "But I can understand that
when somebody has been with the show for a while,
they want to go out and try other things." Johnny
looked around. "I thought you might like to meet
Craig—we've often talked about him, and . . . I just
wanted to publicly thank him, in front of everybody."
Johnny leaned back and called, "Craig Tennis, would
you come on out here?"

Johnny reached out to shake Craig's hand. "Listen,
Craig, if whatever you're going to do doesn't work
out, you've got a place here anytime [and to the
audience] because Craig Tennis has been valuable
to this show."

On these words, Johnny Carson leaned across his
desk, put his arms around Craig, and bussed him hard
on the cheek.

Although this may *seem* unremarkable—like a
standard display of affection from any boss about to
lose a valued employee—Johnny's brief demonstra-
tion was, to those who know him, startling. It was
open, it was warm, it was sincere—and it was unusual.

Introduction

Johnny's wonderful and the show is wonderful . . . and there are wonderful cameras, wonderful microphones, and wonderful water.

—MILT KAMEN

January , 1968.

It had been three days since I was officially welcomed into the elite corps of "The Tonight Show" staff, and I had still not met Johnny Carson.

True, I was 26, I could be considered a force behind the scenes of a bona fide show-business phenomenon, and even if the work was not exactly the constant excitement I had anticipated, I was still luckier than my Iowa dreams could ever have imagined. Nevertheless, the point of it all was Carson. Carson-the-irrepressible, Carson-the-irresistible, Carson-the-imp-in-Boy-Scout's-clothing—Johnny Carson and The Carson Show, if you want to get right down to it. Being on the team was fine, but it was only Johnny's conspiratorial handshake and slap on the back that could make it *terrific*.

Finally, the moment arrived. I was standing backstage after the taping with the show's (then) associate producer, Rudy Tellez, when Rudy abruptly said, "Well, Craig, here comes Johnny—I think it's about time you met your boss." With that, he took my arm and led me into Carson's path. As I stood before him, ready to bask in his comradely glow, Carson opened his mouth and uttered six words that were to set the tone for an entire era of my life. "So, Kid," he said, surveying me, "welcome to Murder, Incorporated." Then he disappeared.

The Institution

I'm me on the show.

—JOHNNY CARSON

October 1, 1980, marks the eighteenth anniversary of "The Tonight Show Starring Johnny Carson." Since neither the format nor the principals have changed, that makes "Tonight" the longest-running show in television history (with, as Carson points out, "over 390,000 commercials, over 20,000 guests—and 12 monologue jokes.")

Not incidentally, that also makes its host, Johnny Carson, the most-watched personality in entertainment history.

To grasp the impact of that statement, consider this: it is estimated that during his 18 years as a late-night host, Johnny has been watched—that is, doted on, dozed over, rebelled against, and rooted for—by somewhere in the neighborhood of 26,000,000,000 people. His popularity with the cross-sectional public is unprecedented, and his longevity proves it.

Then there are also the economic realities. "The Tonight Show Starring Johnny Carson" is the single most lucrative entity at NBC. And for the privilege of keeping it that way, Johnny Carson is the highest-paid entertainer on television. Six years ago, I heard from two traditionally reliable sources that Johnny made either $18,000 or $84,000 a week—or $936,000 or $4,368,000 a year. The truth is probably somewhere in between, and, no doubt by now, stacked toward the higher end. Running into "The Tonight Show" producer Fred de Cordova in the men's room one day, he volunteered, "In the time it takes me to pee, Johnny has made $5,000." (You can try to compute his yearly income from that statistic yourself.)

But for another sort of impact, consider this: it is also estimated—this time by me—that not one soul out of the millions who regard themselves as Johnny's fans has any idea of what's really going on behind that familiar face. For being the most exposed individual on television, Johnny is also the most closeted—and while he seems to be the essence of jocularity, he is, in fact, perhaps the most rigidly a-social personality of his time.

Much has been written about him by outsiders, but Johnny's aversion to interviews has kept all such accounts within the flat terrain of public record. We know that he was born October 23, 1925, in a small town in Iowa, and that he was the eldest son of a moderately successful and staunchly traditional Protestant family. His first acting experience was as a bee in a grammar school play, and his first television performance was on closed-circuit at the University of Nebraska (he played a milkman in "The Story of Undulant Fever"). Actually, his career as an entertainer progressed far more smoothly than most, at least he didn't have to work his way up doing one-night stands in the grimy little dives of Boston or Atlantic City, tossing out shtick, introducing strippers, and getting booed off the stage by drunks. But for some reason, he likes to recount the times when, as kid-magician The Great Carsoni, he worked in Nebraska chicken hatcheries and later in Bakersfield, California, where the audience came in with Casaba melons under their arms —but the truth of it is, he was never plagued with small towns and small change for very long. He went straight from school into radio broadcasting, and from there to a steady progression of television shows. We know that when he was tagged for "The Tonight Show" he was doing a successful stint as the host of "Who Do You Trust?"—a show which, aside from being grammatically incorrect, was (in Carson's own words) "keeping ABC alive." As I was leaving the show, he gently encouraged me by confiding about his extreme reluctance to abandon "Who Do You Trust?" because it was so secure. He was not confident of success when he committed to replacing Jack Paar, and actually turned down the first offer from NBC-TV. We know that he's been married three times and has three sons, that he stays out of the papers, that he makes more and more money, and grows more and more restless with his work. And that's about all we know for sure.

And isn't that a little strange? There's our old pal Johnny, a guy we welcome into our bedroom every night, with whom we've been through a lot, who can always make us feel cozy even at 1 A.M.—and here we are after 4,000 or 5,000 hours of watching him on the air, knowing less about him than we do about most of those people he interviews for 16 minutes at a time. Actually, it's *really* strange.

Well, what the hell? we say. The guy likes his privacy. We still know him in a way—I mean, you can't watch a person *that much* for *that long* and not get to know him, we say. Well, that depends.

What exactly is it that we're seeing in the technicolor glow at the foot of our bed? From all appearances, it's this: a charming, mildly mischievous, lighthearted guy; funny, but not intrusive—excepting often for his monologues. In fact, he seems to lead a quiet, regular life—nothing flashy. His show is predictable, cute, comforting. Carson himself can always be counted on to pitch it to you just crooked enough, with those same funny faces and lovable, self-conscious moves that you've been tuning in to catch, like a favorite bedtime story, for—has it been 18 years already? And the guests. They always seem to be funnier, more intimate and risqué, quicker with a little inside story than they are on the other shows—probably because Carson is such a comfortable person to be around. All in all, in other words, he's kind of like us—kind of like *we'd* be if we were hosting a small party every night. That's how it seems, anyway. And, of course, that's how it's meant to seem—but that's not how it is.

The truth is, there's nothing "comfy" about "The Tonight Show"—at least for those behind the scenes.

What has happened before the curtain rises is about as low-key as a subway station during an air raid. Instead of an intimate party going on back there, it's a frenzied workshop, glorifying the power of suggestion over truth—it is, in other words, a show. An illusion. What's more, the man we seem to know so well is not only the illusion-maker—he's the illusion itself.

If there are keys to the inner workings of Johnny Carson, they are only to be found by observation, for he will volunteer nothing of himself. There are plenty of unanswered questions: How does he pull it off? Who helps him, and why? But there's only one good place to look for the answers: "The Tonight Show."

"The Tonight Show," perhaps more than any other program in television, is an extension of one personality: it reflects, revolves around, and takes all its clues from Johnny Carson. It is, in a way, the actual moving picture of Johnny's self-image, his behavior patterns, his likes and dislikes; it's a running exposé of Johnny Carson, and it's that way whether he's there behind the desk or not.

Steve Allen, referring to his own guest-hosting duties, once commented " 'The Tonight Show' could be run by a chimpanzee and people would continue to watch out of habit." Needless to say, that was the last time Steve hosted the show for years—but he had touched on a valid point: "The Tonight Show" has a momentum of its own which is irrepressible. What Steve failed to note—and fatally—was that the momentum is no accident.

A Carson Workday

The Tonight Show makes a wonderful night-
light for fooling around, doesn't it?

—JOHNNY CARSON

I've always thought that one of the primary reasons
Johnny has been able to keep such a solid foothold at
the top of the heap is his deliberate, well-ordered way
of life. ("It's worked so far—but God knows why, so
let's not mess with it.")

Everything in his domain—from his marriage to his
houseplan to the setup of his show—has been engi-
neered to meet his needs in the most smooth-running
and efficient way possible.

When he's in town, and hosting the show, his average
workday falls—like almost everyone else's—into certain, predictable lines. He's not required in the studio
until 2 P.M. (three and a half hours before taping
time) and so—unlike almost everyone else—he has
most of the day free. He likes to spend that time at
home, and mostly alone.

Home for Johnny, his wife, Joanna, and her teen-
aged son Tim is a house on St. Cloud Road in the
sedate and exclusive hills of Bel Air. St. Cloud is a particularly hushed area dotted with widely spaced estates

16

which survey, from their blanket of heavy security, the less prestigious "flats" of Beverly Hills below. The Carson house, built in a distinctly contemporary style, seems to be made up of huge glass panes broken only at intervals by natural stone-and-mortar supports. It was previously owned by producer/director Mervyn Leroy, and had been on the market for months before Carson bought it. It isn't huge and flashy like the famous Harold Lloyd estate—at least it's not flashy enough to attract Arab oil money—but it's too large to be affordable to anyone without an almost unlimited income. In fact, it was considered by most Beverly Hills realtors to be a white elephant. The property suited Johnny not only because of its seclusion, its pool, and its architectural severity, but also because it was large enough to allow him to put in his own tennis court and office-cabana-guesthouse. It's in those latter two areas that Johnny really lives.

Virtually every morning he will play tennis with one of a group of buddies ranging from Steve Lawrence to Ricardo Montalban, but most of the rest of his daylight at-home hours are passed in solitude in his office-cabana. There he has a giant, seven-foot television screen on which he likes to view cassettes, watch daytime talk shows, or study video tapes of himself playing tennis with the ball machine (this last especially on days when he has lost a few sets.) A room downstairs also contains his drum set, a favorite toy. (If he gets to practicing especially hard one day and if he feels confident, you'll usually see the fruits that night when he does an impromptu set with his pencils at the end of a commercial break.)

At one time the most peculiar feature of this "office" was that it contained only one chair: a large, throne-like, barber-style chair placed in the center of the room in front of the TV screen—Johnny's chair. If friends or visitors joined him in this lair, they presumably had to seat themselves on the floor.

Some of Johnny's peaceful morning hours are of course spent working, preparing for the evening's show.

Johnny will go through the morning papers or watch the news, looking for current event items he can mold into jokes for the monologue. Then there are the repeated phone calls, beginning early on, from the show's producer, Fred de Cordova. Fred supposedly calls to let Johnny know how the show is shaping up, to run down the list of guests, topics, and features as they are set—but what he's really doing is trying to blow sunshine up Johnny's skirt and get him excited about the same old formula one more time. He rarely succeeds. Johnny can always find something negative to say about any given aspect of any given piece of work, and when he hangs up, his displeasure is usually transferred from Fred down the hierarchical line until the heat is even felt by the lowest-ranking page.

At about 1:30 in the afternoon, Johnny changes, gets into his Mercedes coupé, and makes the 20-minute journey over the hill from Bel Air to the NBC studio in Burbank. He always drives himself. His refusal to use a chauffeur is partly an aversion to the "big shot" image he so despises in Hollywood, but it is mostly due to his strong sense of personal privacy—he likes to mind his own business and he doesn't want anybody, not even a chauffeur, to know what that business might be.

At the studio he pulls into the parking space marked by a sign with his name on it and a painted star on the asphalt. (The sight of Johnny's little Mercedes beside Ed McMahon's chauffeur-driven Cadillac always amused me.) Johnny then ducks into the building and hurries to his office, which is located on the second floor behind the studio control room. To get to it, he navigates down a staggered hallway—obviously designed by a cockeyed architect—until he arrives at a solid glass door blocking the hallway. The door, like a bank door, does not open until released by a button. It was installed to keep away the "crazies" who inevitably try to get in to see Johnny, and his personal secretary, Drue Wilson, won't push the release button until she knows the identity of the person on the other side.

Between the door and Johnny's office is Drue's office. It's small—about eight feet square—and contains the usual filing cabinets and secretarial paraphernalia. The most striking thing about it, however, is that it is jammed with Carson memorabilia and looks like a world fan-club headquarters. The walls are covered with framed portraits of Johnny from news magazines, with ornate plaques and awards, with Johnny Carson *TV Guide* covers, with autographed pictures of Johnny beside astronauts and Presidents—with what, all in all, is a horn-tooting display of such fervor that you'd think it would embarrass Johnny to look at it. It was in actuality decorated by Johnny's former secretary, Joan Verzola, and, I believe, reflects what he thinks of his public image, but not how he sees himself.

Johnny's inner office is about 10 feet by 25 feet, with a private shower and bath. One wall contains bookshelves and the private TV monitor that enables Carson to look in on what is happening in "The Tonight Show" studio without actually plunging into the fray. Along the opposite wall there's a comfortable couch, and a coffee table that bears a few well-chosen *objets d'art*. The decor is all done in subdued, tasteful earth tones. The real focus of the room, however, is the medium-sized window over the couch. The thing that makes that window so interesting is that it wasn't always there. When Johnny learned that NBC had built Redd Foxx a window in his dressing room, he told them, "If Redd needs a window, then I need a window." And he had them cut through a foot of concrete to comply.

Johnny's attitude toward his dressing room and his apparent high-handed manner in getting what he needs from the network was an attitude shaped by the network suits when Carson first joined "The Tonight Show." They had him cloistered away in an airless little cubicle suitable really only for the storage of mops and buckets. But, he didn't complain. A tiny adjoining room was used for the storage of a few music stands, and Johnny asked politely if he couldn't use that room as a closet since there was none in his so-called dressing room. Rather than complying to this easy and reasonable request, they boomed, "No, you'll take what we give you!" Consequently, as he became more and more valuable to the network, he acquired the juice to make demands, and based on their past tact, he gives it to them in the present and will continue to in the future. I once suggested to him that the rarely used space above his office might just hold an indoor tennis court. . . .

Once Johnny is settled in his office, he takes and places a few calls and then begins to brief himself on the evening's guests and topics. Carson reads voraciously, and almost always has read a guest-author's book. If a controversial issue is to be brought up on the air, he will make certain he can intelligently defend the side he has chosen, even though he may not have a deep personal feeling for it.

I am always amazed that there are still people who believe Dick Cavett is vastly more intelligent than Johnny Carson. Dick purposefully selected guests with whom he could have "meaningful" and "literary" conversations. I insist that anyone can do an in-depth interview with a Buckminster Fuller if his researchers have prepared his questions properly. But no one can make an interview entertaining except an exceptional host. And even more difficult than making a scholar interesting is to make a vacuum-brained starlet seem amusing. There you find artistry, not pomposity.

When his "homework" is done, Johnny moves to his correspondence. The two or three secretaries hired specifically to handle his and the show's correspondence supply a summary of the mail to indicate which guest was popular, which was not, or which got no mail at all. All of us at one time or another would sift through the letters, trying to get a feel for what people wanted, but Johnny went about his research in a more scientific way. He always insisted on getting a generous and representative sampling, and he paid attention to it.

After reading his correspondence, Johnny turns to the monologue material and special material that has come in from the writers. Alone, he begins piecing it together, taking the jokes he likes best, adding jokes of his own, rewriting, and personalizing the material to give this jigsaw puzzle of humor some semblance of continuity. The material that follows the monologue—usually something Johnny gets from a magazine or newspaper—also gets scripted by the writers during this period, and also comes under Johnny's careful supervision. Johnny is at least as good a writer as anyone on his staff, but the incredible quantity of material used every week makes it impossible for it to originate from only one source.

At around 4:00, Fred de Cordova arrives at Johnny's office to go over whatever notes the talent coordinators have prepared for Johnny's interviews with the guests, and these will also get worked over and personalized by him. In fact, they may get worked over so totally that neither the coordinators nor the guests can recognize a word of the pre-arranged interview come air time.

Next, the wardrobe people arrive with suggestions for Johnny's clothes that evening. All the clothes in his "Tonight Show" wardrobe are from his clothing line, Johnny Carson Apparel. Carson's appearance, even though people will refuse to believe it, is a standard by which a majority of upper-middle-class American men design their own looks. Carson's fashion influence is literally incredible—and he knows it. He's always getting kidded about his clothing line and how it must be a tax write-off and a total wash, and he just smiles. The fact is, in the first or second season the line was available, complaints were coming in that the salesmen had oversold the manufacturing capability of the line and sales had to be cut back—the factory simply could not produce enough quality clothing to fill all the orders. A gross sales figure quoted at $95,000,000 for 1976 alone makes the venture sound even less ludicrous—and all for a style which most people wrongly assume is far too flashy for the average Midwesterner.

Johnny was also credited with making the turtleneck sweater an acceptable piece of business clothing. When he took it to its furthest extreme of wearing a white turtleneck with his tuxedo in Las Vegas, celebrities and millions of consumers followed along. However, the turtleneck phenomenon was most greatly helped by the publicity following the theft of a carload of Carson's turtlenecks. Because he was on his way to an appointment immediately following the taping, Johnny had ordered a limousine to pick him up outside 30 Rockefeller Center on the Sixth Avenue side. In the car were 24 turtlenecks he had just purchased for personal appearances. It was raining, and when the driver saw Mr. Carson, he got out of the limousine and took an umbrella over to the door to escort his passenger to the car. In those few seconds someone jumped in the car and took off. Johnny didn't give a damn about the car, but he was livid about the shirts, since they were the only ones available in fad-conscious New York.

After the wardrobe people leave, at about 5:00, one of the makeup men goes up to Johnny's office and does his face and neck makeup. At about 5:20, Johnny comes down with the Director, Bobby Quinn, and works with him while his hands get made up. Now that may sound silly, but an unmade-up hand held near a made-up face looks bizarre—as white as if it had been sunk in bleach all day.

At this point, Johnny has begun to feel his nerves. He nods to the few guests who are having last-minute touch-ups, and if they're friends, they will exchange remarks. When he gets out of the makeup room, he walks backstage and paces, getting his thoughts together. If someone approaches him during this period, they're going to wish they hadn't—Johnny hates to be distracted. I knew of only one person who would take the chance of approaching Johnny just before the show began. That was John Carsey, a zany associate producer, who'd developed the knack of making Johnny laugh just before he'd go on, regardless of the mood he was in. I distinctly remember one time when everyone else was hiding from Johnny's obvious rage when Carsey ambled by Johnny and, in his shuffling manner, said, "Hey, how's it going, Johnny?"

Johnny turned on him, growled, "Son-of-a-bitch" and started swearing into space.

Carsey just gulped and went white. Then, rolling back his sleeve and talking into his watch as if it were a Dick Tracy two-way radio, Carsey said, "Hello—honey? Listen, don't buy the kids that puppy. I think things are all over for us here."

Well, Johnny just totally disintegrated at that. He also went out laughing and did a stunning monologue.

While Johnny is waiting and thinking, he listens to Ed doing the last few minutes of audience warmup. He watches the visuals—the animation and guest lineup—on the monitor, and then sees the close-up of Ed Mc-Mahon saying those four words of broadcasting fame: "And now . . . Heeere's Johnny!" Then, the theme begins, the applause starts, and finally, after a two- or three-second intentional hesitation, Johnny Carson walks through the center of the curtains to begin the show to applause that increases in volume year after year.

And Now . . .

This is "The Tonight Show." Why is "Tonight" different from all other nights?

—JOHNNY CARSON

What goes through Johnny's mind when he's out
there doing his act is anybody's guess. One thing that's
sure is this: when 5:30 arrives and the producers, the
writers, and the coordinators have all done what they
can, the bottom line is that Johnny is out there onstage
alone, and nobody is going to be around to carry the
show but him. If you think Johnny doesn't feel the
pressure of that burden, even after all these years,
you're wrong. One of the biggest insights I ever had in
that connection was totally unexpected. It came about
as the result of a spot I designed to educate the audience in cardiovascular health, fitness, and diagnosis.
The trick was to fool all but the most perceptive into
thinking they were watching nothing more than just
another amusing demo. We used representatives from
the highly regarded Arizona Heart Institute to give the
feature credibility. One experiment we did involved
a new technique for detecting heart problems without

hospitalizing the patient. The technique involved monitoring the heart activity over a period of hours, recording it on tape, and then having the reading analyzed by doctors at a later time. The theory was that many heart malfunctions show up only once in, say, 24 hours, and taping over a period of hours is the only way to find out about those disorders. For this spot, we hooked Johnny up, in the middle of the afternoon, to a small portable unit attached to electrodes on his chest. He wore the unit over his shoulder like a purse, and when he came onstage, he explained briefly to the audience what it was and then carried on with his monologue as usual. When he was finished, he came back, sat down at the desk, and let Ed help him remove the equipment. The tapes were taken backstage to be unloaded and analyzed while Johnny went on with the show. Finally, the doctor who had analyzed the tapes came out to explain the results; he had some fascinating news. He pointed out that Johnny's heart rate, which had been a very healthy 70 all day long, had, just prior to the monologue, risen to 150. In other words, Johnny had a *severe* case of stage fright just like any other person about to go on in front of 15,000,000 people. Even after all those years, and after having been in the same situation literally thousands of times, we had clear proof that Johnny was still nervous as hell about doing his own show. Since then, he has admitted to me that it's even worse when he hasn't played Las Vegas in a few months; he will get almost physically ill before going on for the first show. The fact is, of course, that stage fright isn't a negative thing in a performer—the best performers no doubt all suffer from it, and in fact it's almost essential to giving one's best in a performance. Those who say they don't get stage fright are probably either kidding themselves or are so far over the hill they no longer have any interest in what they're doing.

In any case, he has an alarming responsibility out there, and his way of coping with that burden is organization. He is thoroughly prepared—his show is planned with as much care as possible for a non-scripted format—and that's one of the things that can make him feel secure enough to look relaxed and entertain his audience.

It's always amazed me that because of Johnny, the same amount of effort and painstaking detail goes into the show in its nineteenth year as in its first, but you can be sure he hasn't made the work much softer on himself, either. If you have been watching the show since it began, you'll notice that whatever changes have taken place over these years have been subtle: the set seems to have undergone radical transformations, but in reality the configuration of the furniture, the band, the stage, and Johnny's desk have all remained the same. The musical conductors have come and gone, but the essential sound remains the same. Ed has been there from the beginning (in fact, before the beginning—he was with Johnny on "Who Do You Trust?," the show in which Johnny's attitude and interview style were really shaped). Johnny himself is a little heavier through the shoulders and arms—primarily from being in better shape—and his face is a little fuller, but you'd expect that. His hair has gone from brown to salt-and-pepper to gray, and now, just like he predicted, his hair is nearly as white as the handsome mane his father wears. I once asked him if he'd ever wear a rug if he started to lose his hair. Much to my surprise, he said, "Yes, I think I owe that much to my audience." The reason I was amazed was that I've always felt it takes a vainer man to go bald than it does to wear a toupee. But all in all, even *he* hasn't changed much or aged much over the years. It's as though he won't allow even that inevitable variance to upset his established rhythm.

One of the best ways I can think to illustrate his meticulous devotion to structure concerned a problem with the remodeling of Studio 6B at 30 Rockefeller Center in New York years ago. During construction, the show was moved across the hall for a period, and in the temporary studio, the entire set and everything on it was arranged in mirror image of the home set. In other words, Johnny had to come out of the curtain on the wrong side of the desk, look in the opposite direction for the band, and speak to his guests off his left shoulder instead of his right. It took exactly one night to make him crazy. After the first show he raised so much hell the crew was forced to stay up all night and rebuild the set in order to accommodate what for Johnny was a very crucial component to his method of entertainment.

Nothing on the show can afford to be left to chance, and that includes Johnny's performance. Very few of Johnny's moves are fully spontaneous, and one of his greatest talents is in making something which is totally rehearsed appear totally unrehearsed (the sign, they say, of true comedic genius).

One of the most interesting phenomena in Johnny's style, and one of the first insights I had about him, is his cue-card reading procedure. When Johnny has to *obviously* read something, such as the commercial lead-in for a product he's holding up, he invariably stumbles and fumbles through the lines, reading the card so stiffly that it's almost preposterous for a literate man. The first time I really noticed him doing that, it immediately grabbed my attention, because I'd seen Johnny read cue cards flawlessly many times. It occurred to me that he was putting on this stumbling act to make the audience believe that he was incapable of reading a prepared line—to make sure that when he was reading and didn't want the audience to know it, the contrast between the two would be so great they'd think one of them had to be spontaneous. I was most aware of this polish when he was reading from guest introductions I had prepared. He could read them so smoothly that even standing 20 feet from him and recognizing my own words, I found myself feeling he was making it up as he went along.

Actually, the times when he reads straight from notes or cue cards are relatively rare. His sketches have to be read, because it simply isn't practical for him to try and memorize all the lines. But in his monologue, he uses a different procedure. When Johnny has decided on a joke, he will work it over several times until he gets a feel for it, and then he'll go through and underline key words and phrases. These he pulls and gives to the cue-card people, and when they go to make up the cards, all that shows up on those cards to prompt Johnny onstage is a kind of shorthand, a diagram of bits and pieces of jokes. The cue cards are leaned against the railing in front of the audience, where it's normal for Johnny to glance, and it appears that he is winging the monologue from scratch. I think the whole procedure is one of the secrets of the show's apparent "spontaneity"—in many ways, Johnny does arrange things so that he has to recreate his jokes as he goes along.

Another thing about Johnny's style that seems accidental—but couldn't be—is the alarming number of dud jokes in his monologue. If you think about it, no other comic in the business would have the nerve to get up there and deliver jokes, one after the other, that everybody knows just aren't funny. But consider this: no other comic in the business gets into *trouble*—whether it's screwing up a commercial, fumbling a cue card, or dying on a joke—as brilliantly as Johnny Carson. The fact is, he hates just as much as anybody to go—as one of "The Tonight Show's" favorite expressions goes—"into the toilet" with a joke, but he knows he's so funny when he does that he has almost an approach/avoidance conflict about it. He seems to periodically welcome ridiculous, absolutely hopelessly un-funny material. Some of that material is so idiotic that the audience has to get the impression that Johnny doesn't care what he tosses out. On the contrary—he wants to make sure the audience gets their laugh, and if the joke is on him, then okay.

How Cold Is It?

I'm a comedian. I don't deal in issues. Tell me, what issues do you ever remember Jack Benny for? Or Jimmy Durante? We won't avoid opinion—I like opinion. But that's not the thrust of this show.

—JOHNNY CARSON

Johnny's monologues—particularly his topical monologues—are his pride and joy. They are the only really crucial thing to him, and, in a way, they're the main magnet for the audience—he has a genuine following for them. For me, the most affecting thing about the monologue is that Johnny always seems to be able to get away with what amounts to political and social mayhem because of the cunning innocence of his delivery. It's been said about Johnny that his crooked grin and shoebutton eyes are ploys to conceal a quick and deadly thrust. In other words, he knows that you can say anything if you know how to say it.

In looking back at the history of his monologues, I can see that Johnny has very often been the first person to "break the ice" on a touchy or uncomfortable subject. In fact, I remember an article in *The New York Times* years ago that labeled Johnny the "comic consciousness" of the United States, and I think, in a very subtle way, that's right. Sure, there is a stronger, more direct, and, in a sense, a lazier way to achieve the same end, but the bitterness of it turns away as many minds as it captures. Somehow, Johnny makes the truth, bad as it is, a light and swallowable pill. It wasn't, for example, until Johnny started doing Watergate jokes that the rest of us felt that we could begin to laugh a little, for the first time in history, at the preposterousness of our government. He seems to have an uncanny sense of timing about when a controversial subject is ready to go from being miserable to being amusing. Even when things appeared to be at their grisly worst in Vietnam, Johnny somehow found a side of it that could be turned to humor, and I think it was a great relief for people to be able to relax about the horror of war a little, even if only for a minute.

Johnny is almost passionately anti-authoritarian, and most of his strong personal stands have to do with the violated rights of the individual. Knowing this about him, I expected, and was gratified, to hear him start on a series of anti-Anita Bryant jokes following the Dade County election wherein the amendment to guarantee freedom in housing and employment for homosexuals was voted down. I knew Johnny personally had a very solid moralistic streak based on his truly square and Midwestern upbringing, but I also knew that he didn't believe in letting inherited preferences—his or anyone else's—override the basic premises of justice. On the other hand, Johnny always feels that it's his first responsibility to entertain, and he has done his share of gay jokes, although not as many as he has on politics, commercials, or any number of other subjects.

Curiously, the reaction of the gay community against gay jokes was always stronger than that of any other "offended" group. At one hint of a put-down of gays, the mailroom would be absolutely flooded with letters of protest, and the studio lot with files of angry protesters. Second only to the gays in militancy were, surprisingly, the Poles. "The Tonight Show" learned that lesson early on—in fact, NBC has adopted the informal policy that, if a comic feels the need to do an ethnic joke, he must choose to do it about a group that isn't well organized. That goes for guests and hosts alike. As a result, you'll see periods when the show will have a rash of Honduran jokes or Ethiopian jokes or Lithuanian jokes, since it's safe to assume that there are no Honduran, Ethiopian, or Lithuanian defense leagues that are going to pose a serious challenge.

Still, Johnny used to insist—and I thought sometimes rather suicidally—on doing a lot of jokes on the Mafia. Finally, of course, the Italian Anti-Defamation League got hysterical, saying that there *was* no such thing as the Mafia, and that the term, in fact, could not even be used in public broadcasts. So, the Mafia became "the syndicate" or "organized crime" or any number of other commonly used euphemisms. But Johnny still got heat from "upstairs." NBC made a few euphemistic statements of its own, the gist of which indicated that it was not wise for Johnny to use names like "Vito" and "Nunzio" in the crime connection. After that, Johnny was careful to use "innocent" names like "Big Ralph" or "Red," but he made sure everybody knew exactly what he was saying, because, after all, how many ethnic groups have a reputation for putting people in cement shoes and dropping them in the East River? Johnny's only concession to NBC's ire was that occasionally, after a joke, he would add a sort of half-hearted disclaimer along the lines of: "Oh, the boys won't mind if I say *that,* will they?" In spite of this mild intransigence, I never heard that Johnny was either threatened or "strongly advised" to stop his attacks on the Mafia by someone from the organization itself, although with his many Las Vegas sojourns, he easily could have been. It may, in fact, be his experiences with that criminal element that have moved him to expose them, but I can't say. In all truth, though, since Joe Columbo—the "heart and stupidity" behind the Anti-Defamation League—got himself shot a few years ago, there hasn't been much organized heat about Mafia jokes, and everyone is glad to be out from under that charade. Still, I sometimes wonder how stupid the league really is. As Richard Pryor once said in a routine, "I don't ever want to meet an Italian so persuasive that he can convince a black dude to go into the middle of Columbus Circle on Columbus Day, kill the head wop, and then think he can make it to a waiting cab."

However, another series of jokes Johnny did was at the expense of NBC's Standards and Practices Department (Censorship). One night during the monologue, Johnny asked Doc where he had gotten an incredible outfit made of feathers and beads. Doc replied it had been a gift from the Facowi Indians. Johnny and the band and about a third of the audience broke up. However, the assigned censors didn't, and foolishly never bothered to ask what was funny. So for days and weeks after that, Johnny and Doc did variations on the same questions, always ending with the Facowi Indians. Finally, someone bothered to investigate and found out to their consternation that "Facowi" was the punch line to a joke, which, for the uninitiated, goes like this: There was a mean, nasty tribe of Indians who pillaged and rampaged throughout the West. Along with being extraordinary warriors, they were also amazingly sly, and when cavalry troops went out to locate them, they always seemed to vanish like signal smoke. Finally, an enterprising cavalry officer hired an Indian scout to help him locate the Facowi. But the guide was terrified of finding them, so for days they rode through the worst of the badlands, circling and recrossing their own trail until they were hopelessly lost. In total exasperation, the officer rode up to his scout and demanded, "Now, where the Facowi?"

Johnny's lack of regard for taboos carries over to religion, politics, his own network—everything. It doesn't matter to him who tries to slap his hand; he simply doesn't believe that any issue is sacred. That attitude was, I think, responsible for the show's introducing some of the most vibrant and riveting guests who have ever appeared on television. The one that springs immediately to mind is Dr. Paul Ehrlich, who is trained as an ethologist, but whose real field of expertise is population biology. He is, in fact, the man who started Zero Population Growth. The very first time he was on, he was given nearly 45 minutes, and he spent the better part of it discussing how the world population had to be leveled off or there would be inevitable catastrophe. At that time, population control was considered an extremely radical topic—a highly unpopular issue—and Ehrlich's appearance generated mountains of negative mail. However, Johnny and many of the rest of us were in agreement with Dr. Ehrlich, and Johnny persisted in having him on, doing much, in my opinion, to speed up the acceptance of Ehrlich's views.

Though Johnny will fight tooth and nail against the political meddling of the network. and although he will go out of his way not to bend to picketers, demonstrations, or mass mailing campaigns. he will often respond to reasonable and earnest complaints. Because Johnny is very sensitive to people's hurt feelings. if he gets what he believes is a sincere and constructive letter, he will respond to it personally—sometimes even on the air. I remember once he was doing a series of gay jokes around a character he called "Bruce." He received a letter from a woman who said, "Excuse me, but my son's name is Bruce, and I'm afraid that if you continue to call every homosexual you do a story about 'Bruce,' he'll have a harder time with adolescence—which is already miserable—than he deserves. 'Bruce,' " concluded the woman, "is just a nice Scottish name." Johnny actually apologized to Bruce's mother on the air—and from then on chose to refer to all homosexuals as "Sidney." (To my knowledge. no letter has yet come from the mother of a Sidney, but there's still time.)

Another example of his letter-induced contrition was the disappearance of one of his favorite "pay-off" lines —"The heartbreak of psoriasis"—from his monologues. Again, he got a letter from a man who said, "Hey, I have psoriasis, and you may think it's funny, you may think it's amusing, but you wouldn't if you had it. The fact is, it's incurable, disfiguring, and painful—so knock it off with 'the heartbreak of psoriasis.' " Johnny read the letter on the air, apologized, and indeed knocked it off. In fact, from that point on, he even banned guest comedians from doing psoriasis jokes.

Johnny is also sensitive to people's fears, and if he can find a way to make them easier to bear, he will. Back in 1971, L.A. was being hit repeatedly by earthquakes, and the result was a lot of suffering and damage, and even some lost lives. There was considerable national panic over the quakes—particularly on the part of people back East who were unable to reach endangered friends or relatives because of downed phone lines. In the midst of all this, Johnny was of course liberally salting his monologues and his one-liners with earthquake jokes (disaster or no, they were too good to pass up). On the first night, when Bob Newhart was a guest, the two were chatting away when an actual tremor occurred. Everyone backstage and in the audience could hear the tremor coming, because it seemed to start at the back of the studio with a low rumble and roll forward. The people at home could tell something was going on because the cameras were vibrating. Only Johnny and Bob, who were engrossed in a joke, didn't realize what was going on—until, that is, the roll hit the desk and popped it up in their faces. Johnny, being no fan of earthquakes himself, paled a little, but then he went right on chatting calmly with Bob, making light of the tremor and using his amused and nonchalant air to help set to rest the minds of those people who thought that California earthquakes were something akin to the end of the world.

The big earthquake had so shaken up "The Tonight Show" staff that when the show was moved to Los Angeles in 1972, some members chose to stay in New

York, because of their newly acquired fear. In 1971, however, virtually everyone on that trip was staying at the Sheraton Universal Hotel just a few miles from the studio. Fortunately, it was a high-rise structure that had been built with earthquakes in mind, so it rode out the quake with very little damage to anything except the mental stability of its occupants. When it struck at about 6 A.M., I was sound asleep on the seventeenth floor. At that moment I did one of those things people do when dreaming—I incorporated the phenomenon into my dream, just as I would have done if a ringing telephone had disturbed me. As the quake began, I awoke from the dream, in which I'd thought someone had let a huge sheepdog into the room, and it was jumping around next to me, because the bed was actually bouncing very much in that manner. When I totally woke up, I knew what it really was, so I leaped out of bed and ran to my windows, which faced out in two directions from my corner suite. Incidentally, that's the dumbest and most dangerous thing to do. But from there I could see the water sloshing out of the hotel swimming pool and people in their underwear running out into the patio area. Off the other corner, people were streaming out into the parking lot with towels wrapped around their waists. and farther out in the San Fernando Valley, telephone transmitter poles exploded in the darkness as they shorted out. They would go in sequences of different colors, like magnesium flares.

Twenty minutes later I got a call from a staff member, asking, "Are you all right?"

"I said, "Yes, I'm fine, I'm asleep."

The staff member said, "So what are you doing up in your room?"

"Well," I answered, "I see no point in getting up. It's still very early and I have to work later, and so do you. Good night."

A bit later the production assistant, Patty Taylor, called me. "Goddamn it! Everyone is down here in the lobby shaking in their slippers, and if we're all here, then you've got to be, too!"

I grudgingly got up and wandered down the emergency stairs to the lobby. No one on the staff had gotten completely dressed, some were barefoot, some shirtless, some in bathrobes, and some in tears. Patty Taylor could be seen wearing only her full-length mink coat, each of her hands clutching her favorite pieces of jewelry. Doc sat quietly, not talking to anyone, with his trumpet clutched protectively under his arm. Ed McMahon and talent coordinator Shirley Wood were at the front desk, loudly demanding that the night manager open the bar. Everyone seemed to require the reassurance of conversation and was talking incessantly, except for one writer who was so chicken he'd refused to come to Los Angeles by plane, and had taken the train, instead. All he could do was shake and make wimpering noises. Not everyone made it to the lobby, however. Writer Nick Arnold sat up in bed and watched his friend Bobby Alto, who was staying in the next room, madly trying to get both his feet into one pants leg. "Bobby," Nick comforted, "we have only two choices here. We can either rush down to the lobby and wait for 20 stories of the hotel to fall on us, or we can stay right here and fall on top of the people who panicked. So go back to bed."

The following night Walter Matthau was a guest, and as was the case, for days afterward, each guest had his own little earthquake story to tell. Basically what Walter said was this: "I'd been suffering from constipation for days and I finally got time away from the set to go to my doctor for some help. He gave me some new experimental pill, advising me only to take them just before going to sleep. So I did; then about five in the morning I woke up with this feeling of urgency. I had just gotten myself seated on the throne when the earthquake started. My first thought was: 'My God, these pills are incredible!' "

We'll Be Right Back
After This Message . . .

> You can hardly say *anything* these days
> without getting into trouble.
>
> —JOHNNY CARSON

One of Johnny's greatest pet peeves is the totally pedestrian mentality which inspires the average television commercial. Now, it seems that the average television commercial is written by people who possess what I could only call a paper-straw view of the world. I've always envisioned them as prisoners in little windowless boxes where they receive absolutely no input from the real-life world—and where they sit and work, day after day, on those two lines of copy that will theoretically run sales for their individual client's product up into the millions. They seem to regard television programs as nothing more than elaborate and inconvenient bridges between commercials, and what's more, they have no detectable sense of humor. Their credo is that all ad copy is suitable for carving in granite. Also, there is always one, and only one, proper way to read it. That responsibility falls on the shoulders of a busy entertainer who's got other things to think about—namely, making his audience enjoy themselves. The problem with copy is often that the ad man gets so involved in his own verbosity that the pitch can be almost impossible to read—not to mention being totally ineffectual. So, on many occasions, Johnny will—with the help of Ed—rewrite and fix up both the internal copy and the lead-ins. On top of that, Johnny will intentionally stumble over or camp up the lead-ins, trying to make the crass commerciality of the pitch at least somewhat amusing for the viewer. Needless to say, the ad men go berserk—but Johnny feels it's his obligation, during the 90 minutes he's on the air each night, to find humor in things, and if he sometimes sees fit to do that at the expense of the products and sponsors paying for the show, then so be it. His attitude is that life is easier to take if you can laugh at it, and so he has no time for people who are more concerned about their 30-second spots than about the usually dismal state of the world. Fortunately, "The Tonight Show" spends its entire season being sold out of commercial space and wait-listed, because there have been times when Johnny seemed to be going through sponsors like spare change.

It's always been *Ed's* role to treat the products with great seriousness and respect, and that frees Johnny to be a little more playful about them. Although Johnny is smart enough never to come out and simply knock a product, his irreverence has gotten him into more than one scrape on the air. His more harmless quips run along the lines of holding up an empty cereal box and then wondering out loud about how cheap a company had to be to send him an empty box to hold up—he felt that he was perfectly strong enough to lift a full box of cornflakes by himself.

I remember another time, though, when Johnny was supposed to be selling one of those individual hamburger grillers in which a ball of meat gets pressed between two electrical paddles and comes out as a grilled hamburger in no time at all. Johnny seemed to think that the device had to be an ecological disaster—

that it probably took more energy to cook one hamburger that way than to do a whole batch in a frying pan. The advertising people, of course, were gravely offended and told "The Tonight Show" advertising department, "Okay, we'll show you what a great and economical product this is—we'll come over there and cook up some hamburgers. You invite the entire staff for lunch."

Well, about 40 people arrived at the studio thinking that this huge, wealthy manufacturer would certainly cook up plenty of hamburgers and maybe even have a potato chip or two for everyone. But, in fact, for all these 40 people, the representatives cooked exactly two hamburgers and cut them into little tiny pieces. They had proved in our minds how economical they were; *economical,* yes—the company was cheap as hell.

There was another incident, some years ago, when the Corning Glass Company was putting out a new line of product—a very attractive china which was advertised as being break-resistant (which is obviously somewhat different from being break-*proof*). Well, that was exactly the kind of advertising distinction that Johnny didn't understand, and so he said, "Well, if it's break-resistant, then let's prove it." And so, to help sell the product, he took one of their cups off the desk and dropped it onto the floor. Now, in the studio in New York, the floor was covered with a three-foot-by-three-foot battleship tile, which was slightly harder than diamond. So the cup broke into a million pieces. The audience got hysterical. Johnny appeared to be absolutely mortified, and to prove it was only a fluke, he threw off another one. It broke, also. Of course, the audience loved it, and before the commercial was over, Johnny had broken three or four cups on the tiled concrete floor, and we had another sponsor that decided it would be wiser to invest its advertising dollars elsewhere.

Another time, years ago, one of our key sponsors was Sara Lee Products, a real up-and-comer. During one of their commercials, Johnny suddenly popped up with, "Hey—who is this Sara Lee person? I'll bet she's some drunken old bat in a kitchen somewhere in Des Moines." Unfortunately, it turned out that not only was Johnny in error, but that the president of Sara Lee (a division of General Foods) was watching that night—and, worse yet, the company had been named after his beloved daughter. The man was of course enraged at his product being mocked, but he also felt that the joke was a personal indictment of his own family. To make the story short, Sara Lee no longer saw fit to continue its sponsorship of "The Tonight Show" and its hooligan host.

Unfortunately for the sponsors, who would like the host to do more than just introduce their offerings, Ed McMahon does more advertising of products on the show than does Johnny. Ed's biggest and most regular on-air account is for Alpo, and those commercials—which are literally done live—are always moments of terror both for Ed and the sponsor, since no one ever really knows if the dog's teeth are going to choose Ed's hand or the food in the bowl, or neither. The best Alpo incident that I ever saw—both from the show's *and* the sponsor's points of view—was one time when at the last minute, the proverbial hungry dog actually could not be found. Ed went out and tried to read the commercial, anyway, but it was a tough moment. Suddenly, Johnny crawled into the picture on all fours, pretending to be a puppy and licking Ed's hand. Of course, it turned into a brilliantly funny commercial. So—what else? The yo-yos in the advertising department at Alpo called up right away, wondering if Johnny wouldn't be willing to do that bit regularly. And you wonder why he gets crazy over ad men.

Some Dumb Stunts

[Mr. America]: Remember, Johnny, this
    body is the only home you'll ever have.
[Johnny Carson]: Well, it's kind of messy
    at the moment, but there's a woman
    comes in once a week and cleans it out.

Like most performers, Johnny Carson is vain. He prides himself on his tan, his clothes, his physical condition—and with good reason: he's in incredibly good shape. For example, during the Arizona Heart Institute spot (when the rest of us were busy being delighted with the fact that Johnny had stage fright), Johnny was puffing up under the knowledge that he did not, like most entertainers, suffer from high blood pressure and the kind of stress that causes heart disease. His internal fitness was a source of real pleasure for him. Actually, smoking as he does, he should be worried. However, Johnny is a master rationalizer, and when confronted with a habit like smoking, which is at odds with his physical fitness mania, he says—and believes—something like, "My doctor says smoking is okay for me—I can keep smoking. For some people, you know, smoking is all right with their metabolisms."

In case you haven't noticed, Johnny doesn't mind showing off his physical prowess—or his physique, for that matter—on the air. This is not as true today as it was five or six years ago; Johnny has not only calmed down and matured, but he's also grown reluctant to lay his life on the line just for the hell of it (unless, of course, you count the nightly monologue). Still, in the annals of "The Tonight Show," there are a host of athletic spots involving Johnny that exist only because I was able to appeal to his physical vanity. That vanity was fine with me, since I'm a frustrated athlete and was constantly thinking of death-defying spots I wanted to see executed on the show. In fact, anytime there was a spot that seemed to put Johnny into harm's way—a situation he always plays off brilliantly—it was probably instigated by me. The progression was usually that I would conceive the idea, tell it to him, and he would reply, "Okay, you try it first—than *I'll* do it."

Usually he was a good sport about my suggestions, but I can remember two occasions where he was not entirely amused. One event was prompted by a challenge from David Smith, a young adventurer who had been on the show a number of times describing the incredible feats of strength and endurance he had undertaken "for fun." David, for instance, is the only man ever to have swum both the Strait of Gibraltar (albeit in a shark cage) and Hellespont (which he did twice). He did his own Munich Olympics, but with all the events backward and without an audience. David is also the inventor of the Peace Pentathlon, which actually got him on the cover of *Sports Illustrated*. He felt the modern Pentathlon was too much a product of war games, so he decided to develop his own alternative. He rejected the fencing and the shooting elements and determined to substitute events that would put him more in competition with the elements, rather than in opposition to man. His peaceful series of events was outrageously strenuous, but no times were recorded and he competed against no one. To recreate the forces of *air*, he sky-dived into the waters off the Virgin Islands; once in the *water*, he put on scuba gear and swam through *fire* coral. He reached an island and ran across its *earth,* and then swam another extremely hazardous journey through strong currents to a second island. There he rode a waiting motorcycle to the top of the island, finally consummating his victory over the elements by making *love* to a gorgeous young friend of his.

The point is that after all that, David, lunatic that he is, wanted to swim Hell Gate, a bottlenecked section of the East River near New York City through which, depending on the tides, water roars in an extraordinarily fierce manner. Nobody knows how many ships have gone down there—everything from treasure ships to World War II subs, all of them irretrievable. Since Hell Gate is narrow, David ascertained that it would not be a difficult swim once he had figured out that exact moment at which the rising tide slowed down the river and quieted the currents. The capper was, he wanted *Johnny* to swim it *with* him. So, of course, I passed the idea along to Johnny. His response was that I was totally insane to even suggest such a thing to him, and he was quite possibly right. In any case, it became a running gag of his to remind me, every time I suggested a questionably dangerous athletic spot for him, that I was the maniac who wanted him to swim Hell Gate.

Another time I thought it would be funny to suggest a demo that was totally unreasonable, but I pushed the joke too far and he wound up angry. In the *Los Angeles Times* one day, there was an article about a circus cannon for sale, and the article went into the history of the cannon—that it had been in one family for three or four generations, and all the family members had made their living being shot out of it at circuses and fairs. The article also contained a long list of all the broken heads and bones the people had inevitably suffered. I showed the article to Johnny and suggested, with a straight face, that perhaps we could lease this cannon and shoot him out over the audience, catching him in a net at the back of the studio. At first he assumed that I was joking, but I was persistent with it and he finally got so ticked off that I had to admit that, no, it was not really a terrific idea.

The most agitated I ever saw Johnny prior to doing a stunt was when I had convinced him to do a fall with a young stuntman named Dar Robinson. Dar has doubled for everyone from Steve McQueen to Dustin Hoffman, but his claim to fame was that he had the record for the longest fall in stunt history—some 11 stories off the top of a building, into an air bag. The air bag was an invention some man was trying to sell to fire departments because he believed that anyone stuck in a building, at a higher level than ladders could reach, would be able to jump into an air bag with higher chances of survival and lower chances of injury than into a hand-held fireman's net. The bag was supposedly of such a quality that someone could jump from "infinity" and not be hurt—and, true, it *is* a remarkable invention—but you still have to hit it to guarantee that you won't hurt yourself. Johnny came into the studio during the afternoon and we set up an 18-foot scaffolding and let Dar do a series of simple dives into the bag. He went head first, tucking at the last moment to take the impact on his shoulders and back. Johnny wanted to see me do a couple of these, and I agreed. My first few were done landing on my seat, and somehow those turned out to be more nerve-wrecking because I couldn't see where I was going. I ultimately did two or three head-first falls for Johnny, and he got a huge kick out of it. However, remember that the platform is 18 feet high—and if you're another six feet tall, as Johnny and I are, you are now jumping from 24 feet. That's a helluva long way to throw yourself into something other than water, which is the only experience that I had had at that height before. Even with water, if it's 22 or 24 feet, I personally don't like it.

Nevertheless, it got to be quite a "rush," and after I had done it several times, Johnny seemed to have enough confidence to try. The spot on the show went along fine. We showed a clip of Dar doubling for Zalman King, killing himself at the end of a feature, and then Dar went over and did a dive. Now Johnny, during afternoon rehearsal, had only gone up halfway, doing a seat drop from about ten feet—and doing a lot of weird "shtick" along with it. In the actual spot, he was standing 18 feet plus his six, and there was no question in anybody's mind that he was nervous about it. As a matter of fact, that was the only time I thought I was going to see him back away from doing a stunt. He did a few jokes up there—things like he realized this must be how Wilt Chamberlain felt when he went to bed—and, in fact, he stalled so long that it looked like he was talking himself out of it. Later I found out that while all this preparation was going on, Barbara Howar, who was sitting in the green room, suddenly said to veteran talent coordinator Bob Dolce, "Go out and stop him. I have a very bad feeling about this. I'm never wrong about this sort of thing. He's going to kill himself—go stop him."

Well, whether or not you like Barbara Howar's writing, that gives you an idea of the accuracy of her premonitions. Johnny finally prepared himself, the drummer started the drum roll—which only made Johnny more nervous—and finally it got very quiet in the studio. Those of you who saw this show or highlights from it on subsequent anniversary shows know that he then dove and rolled forward, hitting the bag not quite in the center but a bit forward, while the thin mattress on top of the bag curled over his head. It looked like he had nearly missed the mattress altogether, and the close-up of his face showed an amazed expression of "I have somehow managed to triumph over the ultimate indignity and I *will* go on for another show."

Later on, I got him into a spot which I thought had great potential. That was a stunt where he was taught to breathe fire—*i.e.,* he would take a small mouthful of kerosene-gasoline mixture, spit it out in a spray like a child, causing it to vaporize, and as the gas crossed a flame, a huge ball of fire would appear in front of his mouth. The spot did not come out funny —simply because Johnny flat out didn't like doing the spot, and it was obvious to everybody.

Possibly the funniest piece along those lines was done with a certain M.D.-professor, an expert in pain-threshold improvement. It was an ideal spot for Johnny, because he was put through electric shock and flame and so forth to see how much pain he could tolerate—and he couldn't tolerate much. The payoff to the spot came when this professor, who was also a karate expert, went to show Johnny how to break a pine board with his head. Johnny, who had had a little judo and karate training, agreed to try it. The man, the authority, was quite obviously apprehensive, because he was scared as hell that Johnny would not "follow through." The trick, apparently, to breaking a board with your hand, your foot, or your face is the follow-through. One is not to *bump* against the board, but to think of it as being six inches farther away, and then move as if it's *that* point you're trying to hit. But if you do that and the board doesn't break—let's face it, it hurts. So, Johnny took a little practice chop and the board went "thunk" in a hollow way on his forehead. Then, the guest became truly apprehensive. On the second try, Ed held one side of the board, the professor held the other, and Johnny put his head very neatly through the center of the board. Of course, Johnny then appeared to go into a state of semi-consciousness and for the next few minutes wandered around the stage looking dazed.

There was more than one time when Johnny's canniness about what would play well for him in terms of laughs put him in a position of actual physical peril. I once booked a young boy who was the champion horseshoe pitcher in the U.S. at the time. Horseshoes are heavy, and pitching them is a downright grueling sport requiring painstaking accuracy and great strength. To liven up the kid's spot, I decided to have him do stunts involving Johnny as a target. The boy first had Johnny stand behind the steel peg. He then let fly with a horseshoe that sailed about 40 feet in a high trajectory and landed—thump!—right on the peg. Now, it had already been established that the horseshoes were of such a weight that they could break a leg if they hit you, and Johnny was doing incredible takes throughout the performance. Next, the boy told Johnny to kneel in *front* of the peg, but cautioned that if he let out a yell, Johnny should flatten out immediately. The horseshoe arched over Johnny's back and again was a ringer. Then, the kid told Johnny to kneel *over* the stake—straddling it, and facing the incoming horseshoe—and this is the point at which Johnny almost backed off. If the horseshoe came over a bit too high, Johnny wouldn't have been able to get out of the way, and he'd have gone from baritone to tenor in ten seconds. Nevertheless, he stayed, and the horseshoe again clanked home. The finale was an incredibly nervy stunt wherein Johnny placed his chin on top of the stake, no more than 18 inches from the floor. After an endless moment of hesitation, the boy did sail it in as a ringer, but I can tell you that my life flashed before my eyes as I saw this monstrous steel object flying through the air straight for the face of our star and bill-payer.

Another close call, both for Johnny and for my future on "The Tonight Show," came in 1968 when Bill Toomey, the former Olympic decathlon gold medalist, was to appear on the show. I had known Bill from college at the University of Colorado, and by phone Bill and I agreed that Johnny should compete with him in a few of the decathlon events. Johnny, competitor that he is, wasn't so sure he'd be badly outclassed, so —to my delight—he agreed. They both showed up in their track suits in front of the cameras at a little college in the San Fernando Valley for the big "jock-off." The last television event was the 100-yard dash. It was a big surprise: Bill confided to me later that he was expecting to just be able to loaf along, but Johnny was so quick he found himself really pushing to beat him. When they had finished the race, director Bobby Quinn asked them to do the dash a second time, so he could get the whole thing from another angle. At first they stared at him in disbelief, but eventually they set off. This time, Johnny really pressed to get up with Bill, and he nearly made it, too —but in pushing, he fell and, just like a little kid, skinned his elbows and knees very badly. For days afterward he walked around stiff-legged, and whenever he sat down he'd carefully pull his pants legs away from the scabs on his knees. I was, needless to say, mindful not to be too much in evidence during that period.

Perhaps the best regular stunt feature I developed for the show involved one of the nicest ladies ever to appear on it—Joan Embry, an animal handler at the San Diego Zoo. I remember getting that first call from a press representative for the zoo, asking if we would be interested in an animal guest. I was a bit reluctant at the time, but said, "Oh, sure, I'll be glad to meet with her if she can come up to L.A." So, on one of our trips to California, Joan Embry came up and we sat and chatted. It was instantly apparent to me that Joan had no professional training as a spokeswoman or as a performer, but she had the totally natural instincts of a totally natural human being, and she was quickly booked on the show. I can remember the first time she was on, one of the animals she brought with her was a young elephant named Carol that she'd taught to paint. This elephant picked up a brush with her trunk, dipped it into a bucket of paint, and then "created" a mural on the floor. Of course, she got paint all over Johnny. It was a hysterical spot and turned out to be the first of many, since I made the joyous discovery that the only time Johnny didn't mind being upstaged was when he was being upstaged by an animal.

Of all the animals Joan eventually brought, ranging from tigers to rhinos to orangutans, the one that undoubtedly caused the most revulsion and fear—even in Joan—was a tarantula. Now, one of the things Johnny always does best is to appear terrified and shocked by animals, which, in fact, he is not at all. In this case, however, I think he was somewhat re-pulsed. Joan managed to pick it up and put in on Johnny's hand, where it walked around and up his arm to his bare neck. Joan explained that this was a relatively small tarantula—only about four inches in diameter—but its relatives can grow to a body length of two inches and a leg spread of nine inches. Joan calmly explained to Johnny that the tarantula actu-ally has to be deliberately annoyed before it would sting, and even then its sting would be no worse than that of a wasp—painful, but hardly fatal. Johnny watched the spider with apparent horror and then asked, right on cue, "Exactly what kind of thing might I do that would annoy it?"

Johnny always liked to see Joan bring elephants on the show—not only because he rather liked them, but because he had learned very early on that if he put a handful of peanuts in his pants pockets, the elephant would smell them and keep going for Johnny's crotch with his trunk.

Crazys and Crackpots

I don't think I'm a great deal happier now than I was back in Nebraska.

—JOHNNY CARSON, 1966

Although Johnny doesn't seem to mind risking his life to thrill 15,000,000 strangers on a talk show, the fact is, he is concerned about his personal safety off the air.

He is not fond of being approached or gawked at by people he doesn't know, regardless of whether or not they are worshipping fans. A special and deep-rooted fear of his is the phenomenon of Hollywood tour buses, the kind that take sightseers on tours of stars' homes. To Johnny—and most other celebrities victimized by these companies—this is not only the height of rudeness, but it's dangerous, as well. Getting robbed, threatened, and extorted because everybody and his uncle know exactly where your home is does not help to make the life of a public figure amusing. A couple of years ago, a fan—just a regular kid, unarmed and apparently harmless—climbed over the fence around Johnny's house and tried to get a look at him. Johnny spotted him, grabbed a handgun, chased him down, and made him stand against a wall, spreadeagled until the police came.

But to my knowledge, there has been only one serious attempt made on Johnny's life (movie stars are constantly being threatened), but I don't think he's ever really gotten over it. It was Joanna who gave me most of the facts from this case—an extortion attempt—which happened several years ago. It was during the time when Johnny and Joanna were staying in a leased house waiting for their new house on St. Cloud Road to be remodeled.

One morning they went down to the St. Cloud house to see that work was progressing, since in Bel Air and Beverly Hills you must reportedly watch the workers every minute or nothing gets done except the issuing of bills. Anyway, when they arrived at the house, a painter was already there working and he quietly took Johnny aside and handed him some things he had found that morning by the front door. Johnny looked at them and then immediately hid them from Joanna because, she believes, he didn't want her to be alarmed. However, she said, "What have you got there?" When he turned, she saw that he was holding a pair of very expensive binoculars and an empty hand grenade with a note attached. The note made it clear that somebody was watching Johnny and his family, and that they were in danger. They were also, the note said, to take the writer seriously.

Johnny tried not to appear worried, but obviously that sort of thing would upset anyone, and his first inclination was to call the Bel Air Patrol. That's the same private security patrol, by the way, that once stopped him while he was walking his dog and said, "What are you doing there?"—which Johnny felt was a pretty stupid question. He answered them flippantly with, "What does it look like?" Whereupon, they made a move to arrest him before one of the patrolmen finally recognized the star of "The Tonight Show." They don't like people walking in Bel Air and

Beverly Hills, ever—feet are against the law in these communities.

Anyway, the Bel Air security guards were much more upset about the threat than Johnny was, so they contacted the police, who in turn sent detectives out. The note attached to the grenade said that Johnny had to pay the writer $500,000 or else some member of his new family, which meant either Joanna or her son, Timmy, would come up dead one day soon. The note said that the writer would be in touch with Johnny on a certain date.

On that day, a call came to the NBC studios. The man asked Johnny if he had gotten his package and if he understood what it meant. Johnny said, "Yes."

"Well," the man said, "I'm glad you do, because this is not a funny matter. I'll be calling you back on Friday at 3:00."

Johnny said, "Well, I don't work this Friday, so please don't spoil my day off for me." Carson was beginning to take the man more seriously at that point, but he still wasn't afraid. What he wanted the man to think was that he was ready to buckle under to his demands and let his threats go unchallenged, which apparently was a very wise attitude.

"Did the man agree not to call on Friday?" I asked Joanna.

She said, "No, the man said, 'Well, you'd better be in your office at three on Friday, or else'—the man actually said, 'or else.' "

So Johnny went out of his way, and was in the office at three. The detectives had him and the phone wired by then, and Carson waited to get his next set of instructions.

I asked Joanna if the family was being protected and watched at that time.

She said, "Yes, we were all being guarded 24 hours a day. We had plainclothesmen at the house and there were even detectives watching Timmy at his school. One of the men watching Timmy actually worked in the kitchen at the school cafeteria during school hours, under cover."

The next instructions—which the police heard, of course—were that on the day of the payoff, Johnny was to make a routine-looking trip to the bank and there withdraw from his account $500,000. The police then worked out a deal whereby Johnny could drive to the bank and go through those motions while still being protected—he was, in fact, to follow all instructions to the letter in case anybody was watching him along the route. Then he was to go to his office and wait for another call. He went to the bank and picked up a suitcase which, of course, did not have the money in it, then drove to his office. The man then called and said, "You got the money?"

When Johnny said, "Yes," he was instructed to go to Carl's market at Santa Monica and Doheny and wait in a pay-phone booth for further instructions. Johnny went, and waited, and the phone rang exactly as he had been told it would. It was then that things really started to go wrong. The police had men up on top of the market with rifles and Johnny and the phone were both wired. The police even had a third manner in which to cover the problem: Johnny was to write down his instructions on a piece of paper which had a carbon copy on the back, and when he left the phone booth he was to stuff the carbon in the coin-return slot. Johnny did this, then got into his car and started to follow instructions. About that time, a fan of Johnny's, who just happened to be in the market and spotted Johnny, saw him get into his car. So he decided to follow him, just to see where he was going. Where Johnny was going, of course, was to the next location to leave the money (actually newspaper). Joanna was listening to all this happening live, because the police were with her at the house and had a radio that picked up all the police calls and phone calls from the scene.

The next thing they knew, Johnny was reportedly being followed by a red Camaro occupied by "male and female Caucasians." Johnny drove calmly to the drop site and quickly put the bag full of newspaper in the spot specified to him. Almost immediately, a man stepped out from concealment and picked it up. The second he did that, policemen came pouring out of every crack in the sidewalk and from every door and window around, because as soon as they had heard where the drop was going to be made, they had radioed ahead and ordered plainclothesmen to position themselves all around the area. So, the police instantly grabbed the extortionist in mid-flight.

The problem was that there was also this couple, the Caucasians—two curious fans in a red Camaro. All they saw as they pulled up behind Johnny's car was a mass of big brutes, dressed like lumberjacks or longshoremen or hippies, all carrying guns, all extremely unhappy, and all converging on them. The guy driving the Camaro panicked. He had left his car seconds before the bust happened, wanting just to walk up to Johnny and "say hello"—maybe ask for an autograph. Well, the fan thought he was being attacked by all these brutes and tried to defend himself, and they literally "beat the shit out of him." His girl friend, of course, was watching all this happen. She was terrified, so she slid over behind the wheel to try to escape, and in her panic she ran the Camaro smack into a police car, demolishing it. The whole thing sounds like a bad episode of "Starsky and Hutch," but it actually happened. The policemen, who were sick of the kind of anxiety extortion plots put everyone through, were really rough on the couple, even though they turned out to be totally innocent of the plot.

Sometime later, I asked Joanna what her reaction had been as she listened to all this on the police radio, and she admitted that even as dangerous as the situation seemed to be for Johnny, she had been completely fascinated. She felt like she was "living in an episode of 'Police Story' "—which I thought was a very loyal Hollywood sentiment, considering.

Johnny could become, if not frightened, at least very unsettled by the sudden appearance on "The Tonight Show" set of people who did not belong there. The trips to California were particulary tough times for security, because the guards didn't know our staff and they were never sure who should have been there and who shouldn't. So, one time a kid did somehow manage to get backstage, intending to make headlines by running onstage during the show—but he was so dumb that he walked out during a commercial and wasn't even seen on the air. What he did was ask Johnny to autograph a lemon. Johnny was extremely hostile to him, telling him to get the hell out of there, and then he commanded the guards to remove him.

Another time, when the show first moved to California, one of the pages pointed out to me a huge man sitting about eight rows up on the aisle, wearing bib overalls, a farmer's hat, and a red-checked shirt. He was knitting. He looked slightly familiar and highly menacing, so I told the page to keep an eye on him, because he was sure to have something unfunny in mind. Still, nobody wanted to go out on a limb and actually do anything about this guy in advance. Buddy Hackett was a guest that night, and, sure enough, right in the middle of Buddy's spot, this man stood up and started to move down toward the stage. As he came down past me, I stepped out and grabbed his arm to keep him from walking out on the set. Well, the man was so huge he just shrugged me off like a gnat and kept walking. He also shot me a glare that said: "Don't try that again!" That was slightly embarrassing—especially since my work uniform of the day was a very macho set of Levi's and a football jersey, and this Rube had made it appear that I wasn't even there. Anyway, he went on up to the stage. Johnny and Buddy just stared at him, in shock, as he sat down and made himself comfortable. He said that he represented the Burbank Sewing Circle and he was there to welcome Johnny to California. Johnny humored him for a minute, and then Buddy wryly in-

formed the audience that they were being treated to
a portion of the show which would definitely not be
seen on the air. He was right. Johnny politely asked
the man to leave, and as he walked off the stage, the
security people were waiting, backed by the Burbank
police, to arrest him. He turned out to be character
actor Timothy Carey, whom you would no doubt
recognize if you saw; he sometimes plays the roles of
mental retardates and psychopaths. What had happened was that Carey had been unable to get himself booked on the show by legitimate means, so he
had decided to take matters into his own hands. He
still didn't get on the show, of course, since he was
edited out—and, what's more, he had better not ask
anyone for a chance to actually guest someday, because he should live so long.

I believe that intellectually, Johnny is not much
plagued by paranoia about threats on his life. I think
he realizes that a major theatrical personality has
never been assassinated for political reasons—although
Johnny, with his irreverent political observations,
certainly comes the closest to being a target. When
you think about it, the kind of controversy Johnny
arouses during the course of, let's say, 40 to 50
minutes of monologue during a normal week, is more
new material than Will Rogers would do in an entire
year in his heyday—and certainly Will Rogers angered enough people in both politics and society to
feel endangered at times. Most death threats are simply idle, and Johnny knows that. At one time there
was a man who somehow got into the studio on three
separate occasions and made it all the way to
Johnny's office. He certainly was scary *looking,* but
his whole motivation was that he believed there was
a conspiracy to kill Johnny, and he was the one man
who could protect him. He was dragged away kicking
and screaming all three times he showed up. It was
owing to his performance that NBC had the clear glass
door erected in the hallway outside Johnny's office
door.

Back in New York, there was a period of a few days when Johnny would get a call every afternoon just before the show from a man with a German accent who would declare that he had a Luger and he hated Johnny and he was going to kill him on the air. He never thought to give any reason for his hatred; he simply assumed that *everyone* hated Johnny and that he was acting as spokesman for all of them. It made Johnny mildly agitated, but he simply would not allow himself to be intimidated by a phone call. Everyone on the show knew what was going on, and I remember the cameramen and some of the stagehands even delayed a taping one night in protest —a very rare occurrence (needless to say, since they retained their jobs). Somehow, word had trickled down to them that there was a potential assassin in the audience, and they didn't want to be shot in the back. That seemed a bit ludicrous to all of us, since if Johnny was willing to go out there and be a target for any crank in the studio, the cameramen working off to the sides should certainly have the guts to do *their* jobs. I remember Johnny getting a huge laugh from the staff toward the end of the week when, in the middle of one of his monologues, he looked up at the audience and said to the assassin who was or wasn't there, "Well, you might as well do it now—I'm dying, anyway."

Inside Jokes

Johnny doesn't care to do anything personal.

—DICK CAVETT

Much of what passes for the "electricity" of "The Tonight Show" is just the high level of nervous anxiety exuded by Johnny, the guests, the crew, and the backstage staff. But there is another element to it—a game of backstage mischief-making that Johnny bats around under cover, or during commercials. He engages in this acting-up not only to ease his tension, but also to create an air of conspiratorial ribbing that will tantalize the audience into watching more closely when the cameras are on him.

It must be said that Johnny does love the risqué and off-color. That's not an image that comes across strongly on the air, but it's always there as an undercurrent, cooking behind the scenes—and encouraged even if tacitly by Johnny himself.

I can remember back when Allen Funt, who's made his fortune with "Candid Camera," used to appear regularly on the New York "Tonight Show." He'd always bring a piece of classic footage to amuse the audience, and the spots were extremely effective. At one time, he was making a motion picture entitled *What Do You Say to a Naked Lady?*. It was done in the "Candid Camera" format, but involved sex as the common denominator in each scene. I went over to Allen's office one day to get him ready for a show, and he said he had a piece of film he'd like me to take back and show Johnny, because Allen thought the man in this particular footage looked a great deal like Johnny.

I said, "Sure." So he gave me some 35-mm film to tuck under my arm. I called Johnny and told him that I was supposed to show him a man Allen Funt thought looked like him, and Johnny was eager to see it. So I had the tele-ciné people put it on a projector, meaning to have them route it exclusively through to Johnny's dressing room monitor. Now, the premise for this piece of film was that they had called a cab to come pick somebody up at a burlesque house in Philadelphia, and when the driver got there, his passenger wasn't ready. So they asked him to please go wait in a room off the lobby. This man dutifully went in and sat down in a large dressing-room area to wait for his fare. As he was sitting there, the doors at the other end of this big room opened and about 30 stark-naked women walked in. The shot is of the man sitting (so it's from waist to above his head), and as he sits there turning absolutely to stone, his eyes staring straight ahead into the hidden camera, all you see is tits and asses of every conceivable shape and size going by in all different directions. Well, the crew got such a kick out of the film that they decided to show it again—all over the studio—so that other people could see it, too. It came up on the monitors in all the studios in the middle of the afternoon. Apparently, it was a great shock to the afternoon tour guide to be explaining to his group of visiting nuns how the monitors work and then to look up and see a parade of naked women going by on the screen. Ironically, none of the nuns complained and there were no serious repercussions—except from Johnny, whose only remark was that he certainly didn't think that the very elderly man in the films looked anything at all like him.

When the show was still based in New York, we used to come out to California for two to six weeks a year to goose up the ratings during the "sweep" periods. It became the custom on those trips to have, after the monologue, some bubblehead in a Frederick's of Hollywood fantasmagoric creation walk out and present Johnny with a note for a commercial lead-in. These girls . . . well, if you can imagine an exaggerated, blown-out version of Daisy Mae, you have a rough idea of what they looked like. Ironically, they were not easy to find, even in Hollywood —particularly as women's lib began to take hold. Any actress with a good face—not to mention a spectacular figure—would not, after all, submit to being just a total sneering sex object, even to get national exposure. Consequently, the women got to be of an increasingly depraved caliber—in general, just "trashier and flashier."

Whenever we'd be using these girls, the staff would outdo each other devising ways to break Johnny up on the air. For instance, I remember one evening when a girl came out with the word "F-U-C-K" written carefully across her front teeth, so that only Johnny could see it when she smiled. Another time, a girl came out with a little note written across her cleavage which said, "Go down starting here." Sometimes the lead-in notes for commercials would tell Johnny what he had to say for the sponsor, and then would go on to suggest various anatomical feats he might perform on the deliverer of the note while the commerical ran. Johnny definitely dug these little jokes, but he couldn't afford to completely dissolve onstage without explaining to the audience, so the control he exerted was considerable. He'd usually do a private take to backstage and manage just enough of a break-up to let the audience know something was going on, but never mind what that might be.

As a former New Yorker inspired by the outlandish flesh culture of Hollywood, I once invented a Frederick's of Hollywood fashion show, to be hosted on the air by Johnny and Dean Martin. I looked forward to sitting in on the casting session with Bobby Quinn, anticipating a veritable extravaganza of parading lovelies as a fitting reward for my brilliant idea. The appointments were set up by a lady from the casting department, and the girls came to be auditioned in her office. Bob and I would go in there, and Bob would sit down with each girl, look at the photographs she had brought, study her, and chat with her briefly—all in a very businesslike fashion (which, I can tell you, was a great disappointment to me after hearing all the outrageous stories about casting-couch "depravity" in Los Angeles). Not one of the girls we saw was terribly gorgeous or special, but enough of them were sufficiently flashy to at least bring off the effect of the "highly revealing" Frederick's fashions. So much for my dreams of naked glory.

The fashion show itself went off with no small amount of hysteria, not to mention repercussions from the NBC hierarchy. In the end, the only people who came out ahead were the stagehands, who were very creative in finding excuses to wander back to the changing area to get in on what amounted to a free strip show. It was funny to see the lighting rails aloft the backstage area crawling with men who wouldn't, under normal circumstances, even hear of risking their limbs up there, although it was technically part of their regular jobs.

There was, I admit, one time when the temptation of hiring prop girls got me embarrassed on the air. On a vacation in Acapulco years ago, I was sitting in a discothèque when I spotted a very, very pretty little blue-eyed blonde sitting at the adjoining table. She was in the company of a man whom she introduced as her father—and who, incredibly enough, actually *was* her father. She was 18 to my wild-eyed 28; we danced a few times, and then got to talking. Now, it's not that

I was looking for an angle, you understand, but the thought did strike me that she wouldn't look bad on television, and it couldn't hurt my position to mention that fact—with me as the obvious tie-in. So in a tequila fog I casually interviewed her. Well, she was no intellectual giant, but she *was* able to read and write to some extent, and, what was more, she was at that time the reigning Miss Palm Springs. I ultimately got around to suggesting, in my best movie mogul manner, that perhaps she'd like to appear on "The Tonight Show" as a prop girl. She said yes, naturally, and had her father dig around for the business card of her agent—which turned out to be her mother.

By the time my tan had worn off, I had completely forgotten about her and the whole incident. But one day, about a year later, Bobby Quinn came over to me and said, "I think there's someone back here whom you know." And he poked his finger in the direction of a pretty blonde. It took me a minute to remember because I had forgotten all about her. This was the girl from Acapulco and she had, indeed, followed up on my suggestion and had, in turn, been cast as a prop girl.

Of course, my immediate reaction was, "How nice to be able to give someone a hand with her career." And I was quite pleased with myself. Then came that point in the show when this girl came out, gave Johnny the prop, and paused to exchange a few words with him. The conversation meandered around and Johnny asked her where she was from. When she said Palm Springs, Johnny commented that that was very unusual—most of our prop girls were recruited from the Los Angeles area.

Johnny said, "How is it that we found you when you live all the way out in Palm Springs?"

And she naïvely replied, "Oh, I met your head talent coordinator at a discothèque down in Acapulco. . . ."

Well, that was it. Johnny rolled his eyes, smirking heavily in the direction of the band, and in the flurry of allusions that ensued—none of which the girl understood at all—I watched my clean-cut reputation disappear into oblivion forever.

Sometime after that episode, I became the brunt of a series of monologue jokes from which I was never to fully recover (or at least my social life did not). They started mainly because I was the most visible bachelor on the staff. First there was a little joke Johnny wrote one night, but then the writers picked up on it and wouldn't let go. The jokes all hung on the mythical habit I had of dating *dogs*. For instance, a typical joke might go that I had taken my date to a dinner party and she had been on her best behavior all during the meal, but then she spoiled the whole evening for me by taking her steak bone out in the backyard and burying it. Or, using the same setup, Johnny would report that since the girl had been so obedient to me, I had gotten her a special present for her birthday—a Gucci flea-and-tick collar. On Valentine's Day, of course, I had gotten her a matching set of heart-shaped Gaines Burgers. You get the gist. Fortunately, I wasn't the only one on the staff to come under attack. Johnny also liked to point out on camera that "Easy Emily" Marshall, Fred's secretary, tended to disappear from work whenever the fleet came into San Diego harbor.

On Guard

If you say a funny line on his show, Carson repeats it, scavenging, hunting all over for the last vestiges of the joke, trying desperately to pull a laugh of his own out of it. You're better off if you're one of those kooky *dames* he loves—at least that way he can do his takes.

—Unnamed male comic

Johnny's strong sexual orientation carries over into his hosting duties, though the average viewer would never detect that, I think, on his own. Naturally, he loves to interview attractive young ingenues—that's obvious. But when the camera is not on him, he can also be seen from the studio casting surreptitious glances down the cleavage of any guest whose décolletage permits. The closest I've seen Johnny come to admitting to this tendency was recently, when country singer Dolly Parton was a guest on the show. Johnny had obviously decided that interviewers had been backing away, as it were, from the glaring issue of Dolly's chest for too long. He was going to brave the waters. After a few blushing moments tiptoeing around the subject, Johnny finally blurted, "Now I

have certain guidelines on this show . . ."—[pause]—
". . . but I would give about a year's pay for the
chance to peek under there just once."

Johnny's strong sexual bent also manifests itself in
another, less obvious, way: he has an uncontrollable
tendency to compete with young male guests. The
younger and more attractive they are, the more difficult it is for Johnny to treat them warmly or even
objectively. If you're watching, you can see it happen.
When Johnny notices that one of his male guests seems
to be really appealing to the audience with an extra
measure of charm and good anecdotes, he will immediately get restless. At first he'll be polite and ap-
preciative, but in no time he'll begin looking for any
flaw in a guest he can do an "eye-take" on. If that
fails, he simply "lays out"—that is, he very subtly
withdraws from the interview and waits either for the
guest to get himself in a hole or for the cameraman
to come looking for him. Johnny can kill a guest with
an arched eyebrow. Whatever the predicament, the
one thing Johnny knows inside and out is how to see
to it that he gets the last laugh.

The only exception to this I've seen is the almost
mystical chemistry he's attained over the years with
Burt Reynolds. When they're on the show together,
it's like two superb athletes conditioned to winning at
all costs, suddenly finding themselves paired together.
I think Johnny and Burt would gladly give up their
whole identities, but only if they could change places
with each other.

If Johnny has a tendency to compete with male
guests in general, the problem gets *really* aggravated
when the male guest happens also to be a comic. It's
a situation so obviously fraught with conflict for
Johnny that it can be downright painful to watch. The
nature of the conflict, I sense, is this: Johnny doesn't
quite understand his own success—in fact, he may
even feel at times that he hasn't really earned his success. For one thing, his style is partially a conglom-
eration of the habits of other comics. *Time* magazine

once summed it up, rather unkindly, with this observation: "Carson is master of a thousand takes. He's got a Jack Paar smile, a Jack Benny stare, a Stan Laurel fluster. If a joke dies, he waits a second and then yawns a fine Ed Sullivan 'ho-o-okay.' A sudden thought—either his or a guest's—will launch him into an imitation of Jonathan Winters imitating an old granny." Now, there's no denying the candor of that statement, and even if *we've* forgotten that his trademarks aren't quite his own, he almost certainly has not. Then, too, he never technically "paid his dues"—he had a career full of good breaks, while other comics went begging. The net effect of all this has been two-sided. On the one hand, Johnny is eager to share his incredible good fortune by giving new and struggling comics a break on the show—but on the other hand, he wants to make sure that what happened to him does *not* happen to them; that is, he wants them to get ahead—but not ahead of him.

There was even a predictable routine with young male comics who were introduced on the show: on the first visit, I'd write an introduction for Johnny that would guarantee the comic a warm reception from the audience. If the audience and Johnny liked him, he'd be good for four more appearances. But if, after those four appearances, the audience was *really* getting to like him, Johnny would tend to turn on the kid. It was just like clockwork. He'd begin looking for any little excuse not to book him again—any negative comment, any joke that might be interpreted as too political or off-color, any profanity. If the comic could make it past that spell to 10 or 12 performances, he was usually safe and could count on fairly regular appearances, because Johnny was past the point of being able to disregard him. As I watched this cycle repeat itself, it always astounded me that Johnny, safe and unassailable as his position is, could fall prey to such insecurities.

Carson Peccadilloes

> [Johnny] didn't have *power*. He is generically not a strong stand-up comedian. Johnny is bright, very inventive, and very funny, but he's low key.
>
> —Former producer of the old "Johnny Carson Show"

A study of Johnny's insecurities would probably not break any new ground in the field of psychology —after all, it's not exactly news that the impetus to perform is often rooted in a deep lack of confidence— but Johnny is exceptionally deft at making insecurity look like something else, so he's fascinating to watch.

Johnny, for example, seems to take refuge in comedy to an extreme degree. If he's forced to talk straight or just be himself, expressing his own opinions, you can sometimes detect him regressing to an awkward, nervous attitude. That's particularly apparent when he is interviewing a guest whom he considers an important star or a profound historic personality. He becomes shy, overly polite—almost subservient, sometimes. It's clear that he's impressed with these people, and hesitant to speak around them, in spite of the undeniable fact that Johnny himself is the biggest and probably best-read television star in the entire world. On one level, he realizes that—he won't, under any circumstances, put himself down as being a lesser figure than they—but on another level you can see that a part of him is still back in Nebraska, and he's afraid all this isn't true. An illustration of that fear is his absolute refusal to be put in a position of asking anyone with a "big name" to do his show, even if he knows them well. Sure, when he runs into one of the "biggies" socially he might say, "Hey, why the hell don't you do my show? We could have a great time." But when it actually comes down to confronting them, to calling them on the phone and actually *asking* them to come on, he won't do it —even if he's begged to do it by a talent coordinator. He wants to feel superior, or at least on a par with them—and if they ever turned him down, it would be hard for him to take. The average talk-show host is quite the opposite: making the show go comes before everything else. In fact, landing a major guest is often their chief source of ego gratification. For example, I remember a story about David Frost, when he had his show, wanting badly to get Danny Kaye on as a guest. David kept calling Danny and pestering his agent, but each time the answer came back— "No." David wouldn't accept defeat. One night Danny heard a knock on the door of his home, and when he opened it, there before him was David Frost, kneeling in a prayer position, pleading with Danny to finally do the show. Danny, not surprisingly, did the show. Johnny Carson would sooner face a firing squad than do what David did. Beyond the fact that he wouldn't even ask *once,* he'd be quick to go on the offensive against any "big" potential guest from whom he'd felt —or even imagined—even the slightest coolness.

Within the safety of his show, however, Johnny is not at all squeamish about pushing his weight around with guests he considers peers. He doesn't forget that "The Tonight Show" is his personal property, his domain—and he's quick to remind anyone else who might have forgotten. The episode I remember that best illustrated this streak was a little conflagration Johnny had with Don Rickles, who guest-hosts the show frequently these days. It was Johnny's first night back after one of his absentee periods; he was sitting behind his desk, and everything was going along swimmingly. Then, out of habit, he reached forward to touch his little wooden cigarette box, the one that's always at the front edge of his desk. The box fell apart as soon as he touched it—it was broken in about five places. Johnny stopped his repartee in mid-sentence. He stared at the box in shock, apparently forgetting himself. "What is this?" he said quietly. "What happened to my cigarette box?" He stared. "Who did this?" He looked around. Doc, who was sitting in for Ed, turned to Jell-O. The show had stopped —you *can't* let the show stop—so Doc tried to make jokes. Johnny would have none of it.

Finally, Doc said, "Don Rickles—he was just having one of his fits, and . . ."

"Yeah," said Johnny coldly, "he's always having a fit." Pause. "Do you know how long I've had this cigarette box? I brought it out with me from New York. I sit here and hit it with my pencils during the show to keep my sanity." Pause. "Where is Rickles? Isn't he taping here at NBC tonight?" Johnny was told that he was.

Johnny got up, motioned the cameras to follow him, and he stormed across the hall straight into Studio 3 where "CPO Sharkey" was in the process of taping before a live audience. And then Johnny lit into Rickles. He worked him up one side and down the other. Rickles was in shock. He couldn't even muster a one-liner to save himself, and Johnny was mercilessly funny; he out-Rickled Rickles, actually.

When Johnny felt he had gotten his pound of flesh, he turned to go—and then Rickles made his big mistake. Out of long Las Vegas habit, Rickles pointed to Johnny's retreating back and announced to the audience, "Ladies and gentlemen—Johnny Carson!"

At that, Carson wheeled and bore down on Rickles until he was backed against a camera. "What?!" he shouted. "Why do you do that? *They know who I am!* You think you have to tell them—you think they don't know? *They know who I am!*" Then he muttered to himself, " 'Ladies and gentlemen, Johnny Carson' . . . Ladies and gentlemen *Don Rickles!*" and then, purple and triumphant, Johnny stormed out.

Johnny has another secret pocket of competitiveness in him, and it's one I've always found slightly amusing: he resents beging limited just to comedy—he wants to be able to sing, too. I think he believes that singers have kind of a racket going—that they say they are singers and they act like singers and so people *regard* them as singers, but that they're really not that much better at it than the next guy. On one show, he actually got the chance to act out his theory—with Steve Lawrence. Now, Steve is not only a gifted singer *and* occasionally uproariously funny, but he's also a very smart man, and when he noticed Johnny making little digs like, "Well, it's just how you come out of the curtains and hold the hand mike and how the band backs you up that makes it so believable," he immediately called Johnny's bluff. He led him over to the curtains and set the whole thing up. Of course, when Johnny came out acting like a singer, everybody started laughing, and he got genuinely indignant—they were spoiling his big chance. He said, "See? They automatically laugh, and it doesn't work." But Steve was determined to see it through, and finally the two of them sang a sensitive love duet to each other all the way through. Johnny was really concentrating on sounding as good as when he sang to the stereo at home, and with Steve's help to keep him on key, he finally had his moment of triumph.

I think the time that he worst feels the limitations of being "just a comic" is in Las Vegas. Now there's no question that Johnny's one of the two or three biggest draws in that town, and he doesn't mind saying so. Although he works Las Vegas mainly for the money, he also sees the prestige in it, and he's one of those performers who will graciously substitute for anyone who is ill, at the drop of a hat (not to mention the six weeks he does under contract every year). When he plays Las Vegas, he keeps track of the house count at every headline show in town, and even though the competition are all good friends of his, he's openly thrilled if he comes out on top. Still, he wishes he could do something different. At one point, he decided to surprise everyone and put some songs in his show. Again, he felt he could sing pretty well— "maybe not as well as Mario Lanza, but certainly as well as some of the contemporary recording artists around." He also figured that if *Glen Campbell* could learn guitar, there was no reason why he, Johnny, couldn't pick it up, too. So he took a few lessons and then, one night, up came the spots on Johnny—sitting on a stool on the darkened stage with a guitar in his hand. He started strumming, and then began singing "Green, Green Grass of Home." Everyone was stunned for a moment, but then, from the front row, came a peal of hysterical laughter. It was Bob Goulet. In seconds, the whole audience was on the floor, and Johnny just gave up. Later, he said something like, "I guess if I had been in the audience watching Bob try to do a monologue, I'd have reacted the same way. When everybody started to laugh, it occurred to me that maybe I wasn't as good as I thought I was."

Besides ego conflicts with male performers, I found that Johnny also has other very active prejudices about certain guests and certain kinds of guests. Still, if he's decided the guest is "entertaining," he doesn't feel his preferences have any place on the show, and he conceals his dislikes very well—unless, that is, you know what to watch for.

Johnny gives out very specific clues about his feelings. He has a kind of body language code that you can pick up. I'm reminded of a column that appeared a few years ago in the *Los Angeles Times,* written by one of the chief journalists on that paper. The man began by reporting how excited he had been to have been granted one of the rare interviews with Johnny Carson, but he then proceeded to devote the remaining space almost entirely to his own reactions to being in an interview situation with Johnny. (He probably had no choice—I doubt that Carson really gave him anything substantial.) Anyway, even though the column obviously related nothing new or extraordinary about Johnny, it was a very entertaining piece. One of the things that I remember most strongly from it was the columnist's comment that someone had advised him to watch, when he was in Johnny's office, to see if Johnny picked up a pencil and began tapping it. On "The Tonight Show," the columnist was cautioned, that always meant that Johnny was bored and about to wrap up the interview. The columnist then related that the minute he had sat down in Johnny's office—before he could even ask his first question—he had looked up and there was Johnny, drumming with his pencils.

The pencil tapping is a pretty good sign that Johnny is getting impatient with a guest or a situation —and there are, if you watch, guests who start him tapping his pencils almost on sight. They'll probably fall into one of a few predictable categories. For example, he cannot bear people who allow themselves to fall into physical disrepair (although, mercifully, old age doesn't count here). He also has an aversion to overly fat and to loud people, and crudeness or coarseness just plain make him crazy. There are also certain people whom he just aesthetically and emotionally can't stand. Curiously enough, though, even if he may feel so strongly about these people that he'll actually refuse to play the same room they've worked in Las Vegas, he is always careful to be polite to them within the context of the show— especially if they have a comedic "rapport" with him.

All things considered, Johnny's probably at his best and happiest when he's interviewing regular civilians. The only people he really likes are "men on the street"—common people with no special stature. He likes them because they're about the only people he sees who are possessed of a little humility.

What Does a Producer Do?

—Johnny wants nothing on his show from now on except guests who are brand new faces and big stars at the same time.
—But that's impossible!
—Not for someone who wants to keep his job . . .

—Producer to talent coordinator

Before Johnny can so much as part the curtains and take a golf swing, there are hundreds of man-hours that have to be spent, every day, toiling in the kitchens of the image factory.

The backstage day has been harried, hectic, and long, full of the last-minute problems that are inescapable when mere humans try to put together a "perfect" 90-minute show from scratch every day. The team that puts it all together—the producer and assistant producer, the director, the talent coordinators, the writers—is as mixed a bag of people as could be found under one roof. There are two common denominators among them—they are all glad to be there, and they are all insecure, creative, and full of bizarre secrets. Every hand that stirs the pot has its

74

personal history, and each quirk leaves its own mark on the face of "The Tonight Show." Let me introduce a few.

The chief quirk, the one around which all other quirks must inevitably orbit, is the producer. Normally, you might look on a producer as a sort of general, marshalling the forces of entertainment. If that's a bit thick, you might call him the show's arbiter of taste and content, the keeper of the creative vision. But a producer operating under the auspices of a personality as strong as Johnny Carson is a different animal altogether. By title and by association, the producer of a show of the magnitude of "Tonight" should have enormous power, and should know enough about using it that his signature is indelibly stamped on every feature of the show. But this is not really "The Tonight Show"—it's "The Carson Show." There's only one reason it's still on the air, and that means there is only one arbiter of taste, one wielder of power, and one signature. What territory that leaves for the producer is tricky to pin down—especially for the producer. He may come in with grand plans, but where he inevitably finds himself is sniffing the wind, playing political jockey, and attempting to anticipate the spoken and unspoken whims of the guy who delivers the monologue. That makes for two sure trends in the center office: bad nerves, and a high turnover. There's even a totem to that effect, a permanent gag furnishing like a progressive trophy that goes with the producer's desk. It's an eight-by-ten glossy of Johnny sitting at his desk, smiling. The inscription reads: "Dear—~~Perry, Art, Stan, Rudy,~~ Fred . . . Regards, Johnny."

The current holder of the trophy, Fred de Cordova, is probably the most fascinating—and certainly the most controversial—figure on the staff, next to Johnny himself. Fred has always been an enigma to me. He is without question extremely bright. He has a talent for charm which is almost staggering. He is *also* dictatorial, unpredictable, mercurial, and perhaps the most opportunistic human I have ever met.

Fred's history is at least as bizarre as his personality, although not on the surface. Fred went to Harvard, with the intention of becoming a lawyer, and he did finish law school, but he never bothered to take the bar exam. In college, he had become friends with one of the sons of the Shuberts, of New York theatrical fame, and managed to get himself a position as an assistant stage manager with them on graduation. He had a hand in several fine productions, eventually elevating himself to key stage manager, and from there it was a short hop into movies and television. I have no doubt that his was a relatively effortless transition; Fred has a knack for divining not only where the action is going to be, but for knowing exactly how to get into the middle of it.

Fred's peculiar personality has always inspired a generous amount of gossip, and over the years it's become nearly impossible to separate conjecture from historical fact. He did not marry until his mid-fifties— which in itself would be enough fuel to sprout rumors in Hollywood, except that during all that time Fred was also known as an avid Don Juan and was perpetually linked in gossip columns with this or that beautiful starlet.

When Fred finally did get married, it was to a marvelously strong woman with a biting sense of humor, tremendous popularity, and a philosophy best summed up in two of her favorite quotations: "Darling, remember, you are not put on this earth to enjoy yourself"; and, "Don't forget, no good deed ever goes unpunished."

Janet and Fred certainly give among the finest and most publicized "A" parties in Hollywood. They share, if rather casually, a beautiful home in Trousdale, above Beverly Hills. It's a massive structure of glass, wood, and stone with a sensational view of the city, and a bathroom (Fred's) the size of which would put most concert halls to shame.

Among Janet's other life-style philosophies in her apparent need to spend Fred's income as fast as it gets into their joint account. I was with them on one occasion when Fred found some humor in her extravagance. We encountered Mrs. Del Webb, wife of the hotel tycoon, decked out in the same exact dress "designer original" gown that Janet was wearing. One dress had been purchased in New York and one in California, and, naturally, the couturier had assumed that the chances of both dresses winding up backstage at the Sahara on the same evening were rather remote. The designer's miscalculation, of course, was Fred's good fortune—he gleefully whispered to me that he could now count on Janet sending the gown back to the designer the very next Monday and he, Fred, would receive a 100 percent refund.

Fred is extremely well spoken and well read—erudite, even. In fact, one of the things that has really, genuinely endeared him to me is that he has returned every book he's ever borrowed. Now *there's* a rare quality. He can be painfully funny, particularly when he's putting himself down—but self-deprecation is a mood which overtakes him, alas, all too rarely.

As for unattractive qualities, his worst is his habit of discussing money in inappropriate situations. One approach he used to especially relish was coming into a room full of underpaid coordinators and, knowing full well how much—or, rather, how little—everyone in the room made, announcing in mournful tones that his bank balance had fallen below $1,000,000 in cash. Needless to say, that was a highly unamusing piece of business. Another of his favorite routines involved telling stories about people who were cheap. These were particularly hard to endure, as everyone knew that no matter how tight the other guy was, he may not have been a match for Fred. His favorite cheap stories were about Fred MacMurray, whom he had for years directed on "My Three Sons." His next favorite concerned Ray Milland, who was a big star in the days when Fred was a struggling movie director. Fred always claimed that when he and Ray went out to lunch, Ray would go into the mailroom and shake down the fan mail until he found envelopes containing change. These he would rifle, and then, on the two or three dollars he would manage to glean, he'd treat Fred to a seventy-five-cent lunch.

One of the funniest stories Fed tells about himself concerns the only time he lost his temper and succumbed to violence. He had just come out of his house and one of those small neurotic hand-fed dogs nipped him on the back of the leg. Exchanging a few belligerent words with the owner, Fred decided to beat him up. Planning to throw only one killer punch, Fred ran at the man who neatly sidestepped him, belted Fred as he went by, sending him head over heels, breaking his shoulder. And Fred could never find the man or the dog again.

When Fred came on as producer of "The Tonight Show," all of us on the staff agreed that his tenure would be very brief—he simply did not, in our opinion, have any insight into the show. Fred followed a popular producer by the name of Rudy Tellez, who was, like Fred, very charming and extemely able.

Rudy had worked as a producer on "The Mike Douglas Show" and then "The Les Crane Show" in New York. From there he took what appeared to be a giant backward step by accepting a job as talent coordinator on "The Tonight Show." He invariably said, when asked to explain this move, "Well, I always wanted to see how it was done in the big time." From talent coordinator, Ruby moved to associate producer, and eventually, on the demise of producer Stan Irwin in a flurry of innuendo, he succeeded to the position of producer. Rudy is certainly competent, energetic, and ambitious, but his climactic rise to producership may have been boosted more than a little by the fact that he married Johnny's (then) personal secretary, Jeannie Pryor. At least that's what the people who were extremely jealous of his meteoric rise chose to believe. Jeannie was a live wire and a special favorite of Johnny's, and she may have been able to use her influence for Rudy's benefit—but even she was not able to keep Rudy afloat in the long run. Rudy discovered he was on his way out in a rather rude, but not uncommon, fashion: his contract was simply not renewed. Nevertheless, he made a laudable effort to see that the reins of power were transferred to Fred, and that fact did much to boost Fred's staying power in the early days.

Fred got involved with "The Tonight Show" rather unexpectedly. He first met Johnny when Fred was directing "The Jack Benny Show." Johnny was a frequent guest of Benny's (although he openly admitted to having borrowed from Benny's material and delivery), and he and Fred became acquaintances both professionally and socially. Fred says he really never had eyes to get involved with Johnny on a show, although he thought Johnny to be extremely talented and "a nice young man." But all during the "My Three Sons" era, he would run into Johnny and his second wife, Joanne, at parties where Joanne, utterly charmed by Fred, would invariably end the evening by sighing, "Wouldn't it be *wonderful* if Johnny would make you producer of 'The Tonight Show'?"

Fred would of course demur and then think no more about it. That routine kept up for years until, like a scene out of some Ronald Reagan movie, Fred one day got a call from Johnny's (then) manager, Sonny Werblin, asking if Fred was interested in the job. Joanne had apparently nagged Johnny, and Sonny then nagged Fred, and after a few months, Fred agreed. (During that era, a stranger must have thought we were working in a kindergarten class, since the three people we spoke of most were named Johnny, Freddy, and Sonny.)

Fred originally wanted to come on as director-producer, but after one day of watching the show being taped, he got—and in my opinion, wisely—cold feet. The quantity of original work that goes into a 90-minute show of that caliber moved Fred to opt for the role of producer only. Still, there is no doubt in my mind that Fred considers himself more than just a producer. For quite a while, a large painting, a gift from the scenic department, hung at the far end of Fred's office. It was approximately eight feet long and stood at least three feet high. It showed the entire set of "The Tonight Show"—the desk and couch, the production stage, the band's area, and so on. The one thing that made the painting peculiar was that the face of every person in the painting—in the band, on the stage, and even behind the desk—was Fred de Cordova's. Fred really loved that painting.

One step down from Fred de Cordova sits the associate producer, Peter Lassally. Peter had a distinctly sad childhood, having been a refugee from a German concentration camp. Some people felt that his sole function on "The Tonight Show" was to remind the staff that tragedy was at all times a real possibility. To that end, he would stand around a lot, saying, "I don't know," looking solemn, and going to lunch with Fred de Cordova.

Next to the producer, the person who was most privy to Johnny's confidence was his personal secretary—a title held for years by a shy, appealing woman named Joan Verzola. Joan took over when Johnny moved out to the West Coast. Ironically, Joan had been Joey Bishop's secretary—that is, until Johnny pushed Joey off the air with better ratings. Joan's chief claim to fame with the staff is that she managed to be courted, engaged, and married without ever having anyone on the show so much as suspect she had had a heavy date. She just came into work one day and casually announced that she was married. What was more, she had married one of the show's own head writers, Larry Klein. Now, Larry was also a quiet man—at least away from the typewriter—but still, the idea that two people could have a courtship in that fishbowl environment and have no one on the staff know about it was truly shattering. Normally, two people can't back into each other in the commissary line without starting an epidemic outbreak of gossip.

The Joke Machine

—Sign over head writer's desk in New York
IT LEFT HERE FUNNY.

Probably the most rivetingly weird characters within "The Tonight Show," both as a unit and as individuals, are the comedy writers. I was always rather jealous of the writers for two reasons: they obviously had me beat in creative ability, and they also made a good deal more money. Whereas I had started at $250 per week and after eight years had only about tripled that, the writers, especially if they were head writers with long-term contracts, could end up making over $150,000 per year. But I must admit that considering the quasi-sadistic strain they were continually operating under, I didn't begrudge them one penny.

Just prior to my leaving, one of the customary "Tonight Show" purges took place, and the longtime head writer, Hank Bradford, along with all the key people on his staff, was discharged and replaced by the comparatively level-headed team of Goodman and Klein. Now, during *Hank's* tenure, it was my considered opinion that the writing staff was at its all-time most cohesive and least sociopathic state—a monumental achievement, if you are at all familiar with the nature of comedy writers. As a species, they tend to hide away in tiny offices where they can intimidate rookie writers, resort to physical violence if someone fails to laugh at a joke, and organize what amounts to a secret priesthood within the show. They succeeded in being hilarious only at the expense of being functional human beings.

A head writer's main task is to marshal the weirdness of writers, and Hank Bradford was a genius at it. His role was to be both catalyst and synthesizer. Hank's head and his humor were totally in tune with Johnny's, and everybody knew it. Consequently, all writers' meetings were something of a performance situation. The writers tempered their humor and wrote their lines to appeal to Hank, and if things bounced well off him, they knew they were on the right wave length. After this "jam session," Hank would sit at the typewriter and try to weave out of the craziness something cohesive to present to Johnny. That little task alone caused him to smoke four packs of cigarettes a day.

(Hank married one of the shows talent coordinators, Pat Silverman, and instantly recast her in the role of housewife and mother. I recently ran into Pat and asked her what the highlight of her "Tonight Show" career had been. She unhesitantly replied, "I once made Buddy Greco sound interesting for five minutes.")

Hank's office was structurally identical to Fred's—but inside it was another story. The decor was about as stable—and charming—as the interior of a hotel room over a downtown bus station. Hank's idea of comfort and order was to have his trash arranged in neat piles on the floor. His bulletin boards were always covered with bizarre eight-by-ten glossies and weird newspaper articles. One of his favorites, which he got from UPI, showed the mayor of a small town opening a new plant. The man was cutting a ribbon of steel with a welding iron and had set his hair on fire. Hank had been a performer himself for more than six years. He'd been on "The Tonight Show" half a dozen times, and he periodically seemed to miss the performing. I'd heard him muse on several occasions that when he'd write a great joke, he'd wonder just how big a laugh he could get with it himself—but as he matured, he concluded that there were more important things in life than trying to make 60 drunk yo-yos in a nightclub laugh, and that's just about what the lot of a moderately successful stand-up comic amounts to.

One of Hank's predecessors, Marshall Brickman (who has since gone on to finer things—notably, co-writing Woody Allen movies such as *Annie Hall*), used to specialize in doing touching little things for his staff. For example, he would have them come into his office early in the morning and, as part of their daily ritual, would make them stand on chairs facing the walls while he played a scratchy recording of the Honduras national anthem.

During Marshall's reign, there was such a constant turnover of writers that one of the coordinators of the era, Mike Zannella, made it a personal rule never to learn the name of any writer who hadn't already been renewed at least twice.

Another pre-Bradford regime was headed up by a man by the name of Arnie Cogan. He has won a handful of Emmys for his writing contributions to "The Carol Burnett Show," and has since gone into producing. Arnie's sense of humor was actually the next thing down from bizarre. He once sent out Christmas cards —the kind you get at the photo store, the ones that feature your favorite snapshot of the family. Arnie's version had the family posed in front of the house, complete with dog, over a greeting that read: "Happy Holidays from our house to yours . . . the Cogans." Well, it was a perfectly straight-looking card, until you let it sink in a minute—and then you realized that that was Arnie, all right, only it wasn't Arnie's wife, kids, or house. It wasn't even Arnie's dog. Sentimental guy, Arnie.

One thing that always struck me about writers on "The Tonight Show" was that they invariably looked like anything but what they were. They looked like undertakers, truck drivers, perverts—but never like comedy writers. One of the best examples of this phenomenon was a hilarious talent by the name of George Tricker. George is huge—six feet, three inches tall, 200 pounds—and he has never been squeamish about using his size for either laughs or plain old terrorism. When you walked into his office, for example, the first thing you'd see was a tall, free-standing metal frame. Attached to the frame was a long rope, and at the end of that was . . . a car tire. What I have just described, of course, is the exact toy found in a gorilla's cage at the zoo. In George's office, this was somehow right. He looked either like a Jersey hit-man or a Manhattan cab driver. In fact, he *had* been a cab driver at one time. Having not embarked on his career as a comedy writer until he was 30, he'd had a whole lot of other jobs, too—he'd worked as a bartender and then a bouncer at the infamous Club Four in Brooklyn; he'd hashed in a lunch diner, worked as a casket-maker, and eventually became an insurance salesman. He once told me he thought he could see the pattern developing there—an inevitable road leading to the greatest odd-job-in-the-sky: writing for "The Tonight Show." His writing break came from Joan Rivers, whom I've always called the manager of the farm team for "Tonight Show" writers. Joan religiously seeks out and gives work to potentially good writers—never paying them a great deal, but keeping them writing and working—and ultimately, when she thinks they're ready, she'll give Johnny a call and say, "Hey, I've got someone whose material you should see." In a great many instances, the writers are hired and, as in George's case, it's the beginning of a noteworthy career.

George was notorious for saying things that, no matter how they were cut, made no sense at all. Hank

Bradford kept a three-by-five-card file of mindless quotes from people on "The Tonight Show" staff, and George was far and away the most significant contributor. He would say things like: "I once nearly killed a man on a door," "Do they have comedians in France?" or, "I once nailed a chick across the street from a Holiday Inn"—always nonsensical things having to do with seemingly impossible feats. These, of course, were always carefully committed to memory to be used against George at a later date.

The story that probably best illustrates George's total irreverence occurred one day when he and Hank Bradford were returning to the studio from lunch. Driving back through the gates they were embarrassed to find they had to cross a picket line which included people like the prop man, good old Jack Grant. Jack always waved cheerfully at them—he had his trailer out in front, full of coffee and beer to keep all the strikers going—and after they had exchanged remarks with him, Hank turned to George and said, "Don't you feel a little guilty about crossing this picket line?"

George replied, "No, not considering the Fuck Crisis."

Hank looked up and said, "What are you talking about, the Fuck Crisis?"

And George said, "Well, that's the crisis there is now, because when *we* were on strike, *they* didn't give a fuck, *either*."

Now, George, who is, as I said, six-foot-three, and big for his size, is downright puny compared to another of the writers on the show, Pat McCormick. Pat is six-foot-seven in virtually every direction. I remember once having to call Pat to get his size for wardrobe, and when we got to his waist, he said, "My waist is either 50 or 54, depending on what I had for lunch." George and Pat once conceived of forming a comedy team (which they were going to call "The Tornado Brothers") specializing in humor through terror. George and Pat liked to go to lunch across the street to a famous Mexican restaurant, Pepe's, for the sheer joy of hounding the bartender, Pancho. Pat, the bigger of the two, used to pretend to be terrified of George—so Pancho figured that if *this* guy was afraid of George, and Pancho was only five-foot-two—well, you get the picture. George used to call over there and ask Pancho in his most belligerent manner who was at the bar. If another of the writers was there, George would tell Pancho he'd better get them the hell out of there—now! Once, Pancho, out of abject fear, made the current head writer, Ray Siller, crawl under the piano so that George wouldn't come in and find him there.

Pat McCormick, of course, is the infamous "Tonight Show" streaker, the one who lumbered across the stage looking just like a great white whale years ago. To give you a rough idea of the rest of Pat's sense of humor, there was the time he was presiding at his mother's wake, when Chuck McCann solemnly joined the vigil. Chuck is a good friend of Pat's and he'd also been extremely close to Pat's mother. Needless to say, Chuck was very distressed and very tearful. Because Pat wanted desperately to let him know it was "all right," he dropped his pants and did a ten-minute monologue.

In fact, any story you hear about Pat McCormick is probably true, provided it's too gross to tell outside of a men's room, and even then, it's probably been cleaned up. I remember a certain surprise birthday party Pat's friends threw for him. It was held at the Polish Legion Hall (where else?) and was done in impeccably bad taste, so you know that everybody there was an intimate of Pat's. In fact, Carl Reiner was the instigator of the party. He'd rehearsed 20 of the male guests for an hour. When Pat was brought in, they were lined up on either side of the door, just like a mock military honor guard. Then on a count of three, all of them, including Tim Conway, Harvey Korman, Jack Reilly, and Buck Henry, saluted the guest of honor by dropping their pants. There were cue cards, so everyone could sing along on "Happy Birthday." Carl

M.C.'ed a Polish raffle in which he'd announce a prize; then someone in the audience would call out their number and win. There were fly-swatters at each place setting. Among the presents were a see-through burglar's mask, and a miniature of the Pièta, complete with its own hammer. They decided it should be a costume party, so you can imagine some of the revolting get-ups. The winner, finally, was a girl who came in a black strapless evening gown with a dirty white bra worn on the outside.

At one point during the festivities, they had Pat break a *piñata*. A *piñata* is a plaster and papier-mâché replica of an animal which is normally filled with candy and small toys and then broken with a stick by the blindfolded guest of honor. When Pat stepped up and broke *his piñata,* however, nothing but gallons and gallons of pig intestines fell out. But Pat was nonplussed. Wading around in the mess, he announced nervously, "Oh-oh, I think I just stepped on Billy Barty [the celebrated Hollywood midget]."

According to legend, when Pat's baby was christened, Pat presented the nude child on a silver turkey-serving platter, all surrounded with parsley. Pat once came to George Tricker's house just before Christmas and was talking to George's father-in-law, who is just a little more religious and considerably more Catholic than the average Pope. The temptation of that piety was too much for Pat—in mournful tones, Pat related to George's father-in-law how he had wanted to go to Mass last Christmas, but all the churches were full, so he wound up worshipping in front of a urinal in the men's room of a Trailways bus station. I hear George's father-in-law offered Pat money to leave.

Pat is actually helpless against the temptation of a gag, and as a result, his bad taste can go to appalling lengths. Once when he, Dick Cavett, and David Lloyd —all three writing for "the Merv Griffin Show" at the time—were walking down Fifth Avenue in New York, they seemed to be seeing a lot of people on crutches and in wheelchairs going by on the sidewalk. Pat couldn't control himself. He finally stopped one and said, "Excuse me, sir, can you tell me where they're holding the F.D.R. memorial convention?"

It must be said, though, that Pat is without doubt one of the best comedy writers in the business, even if he is rather consumed with the humor of bodily functions. He is also credited with authoring one of the most inspired jokes of all time. "The Tonight Show" was in California during the 1971 earthquake, the big one, and for Johnny's opening monologue that night, Pat wrote a mock public-service announcement: "Due to today's earthquake, the 'God is Dead' rally had been canceled."

After Pat streaked "The Tonight Show," NBC made a move to remove him based on a morality clause they have in all contracts binding people in the creative end of the business. But Johnny refused to let them fire Pat—he knew Pat had meant well and was a valuable member of the staff, and has remained so for a record eight years.

Another well-remembered writer was a young and extremely popular fellow, Tom Moore, whose name you can see these days in the credits of almost any comedy show worth watching. No one could look less like a comedy writer than Tom. He's the ultimate WASP. Hank Bradford once remarked that he thought Tom used mayonnaise to groom his hair. Traditionally, you must realize comedy writers are 50-ish, Jewish, and rich; they are also grossly unhappy and have bad stomachs. Their trademarks are Maalox, Gucci's, and fat cigars. Fortunately, there weren't many of those on "The Tonight Show." But Tom Moore's background was also atypical. He is the son of a top network executive—not the usual hard-luck, long-suffering matrix of the comedy writer. Not that his father helped him get his job—he didn't. But Tom did start at the top, in that "The Tonight Show" was his first job after graduating from Stanford. In fact, his background put him in a bad spot more than once, the most memorable of those times being once when Jerry Lewis was a guest host on the show. Jerrry was in his dressing room, and, as was customary, all the writers were marched in to be introduced to him. When they got to the name Tom Moore, Jerry went berserk. He began ranting and swearing about another Tom Moore he knew who had been head of ABC and had fired him from the network, and how he hated the sound of the *name* Tom Moore because it reminded him of that monster. He almost had to be physically restrained, he was so worked up. Tom reddened, but wouldn't have dreamed of saying anything about it. Later, someone took Jerry aside and told him that Tom was, in fact, the *son* of "the" Tom Moore, and Jerry was genuinely embarrassed. He actually apologized to Tom— and I think it was one of the few times in history anyone remembers Jerry apologizing. Under the circumstance, it must have been an extremely difficult thing for him to do.

Tom Moore was only the *second* youngest writer ever to be hired on "The Tonight Show"—the undisputed winner was Jim Mulholland, who was brought on at the shocking age of 17. When Jim started, he was in college and, ironically, by working on the show part-time, he was making more money than the president of the university he attended was making full-time. He started as a writer while the show was still in New York. Jim lived over in New Jersey, and, walking to the commuting train one afternoon after school, he was stopped by the police. They were convinced on sight that he was a grade-school truancy case. When they asked him what he was doing, he said, "I'm going to work."

Then they said, "Where do you work?"

Jim gulped and said, "I'm a comedy writer for Johnny Carson."

With that, they rolled their eyes up into their heads and dragged him off to jail—there was no question in their minds that he was wanted for *something*. Jim had to call his father to come down and bail him out. In New York, the guards—or the "flaky bunch," as they were known—used to regularly refuse to let Jim go up to his office. They simply didn't believe that anybody who looked as young as Jim did should be admitted to the set without a parent or guardian.

One young "Tonight Show" comedy writer who showed promise of developing the traditional Gucci-and-bad-stomach syndrome was Eric Cohen. He initially wanted to be on "The Tonight Show" as a performer, but could never quite get his act together. Instead, he wrote a great deal of material for Gabe Kaplan, and the heart of that became the basis for "Welcome Back Kotter." Eric is a total workaholic. At the same time he was working on "The Tonight show" as a writer, he was writing "The Tony Orlando and Dawn Show" under a pseudonym. He'd have to get up at daybreak, do his "Tonight Show" work, and then sneak away in the afternooon to write for Tony. If Johnny had found out, Eric, needless to say, would never have seen the inside of NBC again.

The tension and lack of sleep seemed to lend its own special twist to Eric's humor. For example, he had note pads made up for inter-office memos that said in the corner: "From the Desk of Adolph Hitler." (Eric, of course, is Jewish.) Eric is famous for giving parties at which he's the first one to leave—that is, pass out. As a consequence, guests often wander out with things like Eric's television set or typewriter. He normally overindulges in everything. At one party he appeared as an Orthodox rabbi with side curls and a long beard. The next time he appeared, it was as a Greek Orthodox minister. Someday he will come as a submarine sandwich, be mistaken for hors d'oeuvres, and meet an ignominious death. At one time, Eric decided that it was a shame that there was no such thing as "show business"—I mean a real business. He decided that he would nominate and elect himself the President of

Show Business. He got an answering service, had a listing put in the phone book, and waited for the marks to line up. He called himself Jack L. Mendel, and, being the President of Show Business, he just had the answering service put everybody on hold and never came back. What, I ask you, could be more Hollywood than that?

Eric is one of the few writers who is truly beginning to understand "real life" show business. At one point, he had actually come up with four or five very well-developed concepts for series, but because he had no track record as a "series creator," NBC always found reasons to reject his material. Eric, it must be said, does not handle rejection very well. He decided to bear down harder with his presentations. Just to make sure he would be noticed, Eric claims he walked into the office of John J. McMahon, director of programming for NBC, West Coast, wearing a leotard, a cape, and a yellow hardhat with a revolving red light on top. By the end of his pitch, he had so intimidated the NBC Programming people that they advanced him a huge sum of development money for what was probably his worst idea—a plot about a pre-Civil War, homosexual plantation owner who was very hep and raised nothing but polyester and had his slaves constantly making him new, prettier outfits.

In June 1980, J. J. McMahon was named president of the newly-formed Johnny Carson Productions company.

Perhaps the most unusual, and certainly one of the most talented, writers Johnny ever hired was Nick Arnold, who went on to produce everything from "Welcome Back Kotter" to "The Stockard Channing Show." Nick is very difficult to talk about because one has the tendency to over-appreciate and even revere him for his incredible perseverance; he is severely handicapped with cerebral palsy. I'm always on egg-shells as I relate stories about him—especially stories that have now become classics, but that also have to do with his palsy. Nevertheless, I always yield to temptation, and Nick never seems to mind. Nick is extraordinarily intense and private, and in most social situations he copes by laughing and making others laugh. The fact that he chooses to ignore his handicap is laudable enough—but his uncanny and unfailing ability to put people on the floor is a mental triumph that can't be overstated.

Nick is another of the writers who was given his first break by Joan Rivers, but he was famous even before that. He was trying out material at the popular New York club the Improvisation, a place where many, many people, including David Brenner, Freddie Prinze, Steve Landesberg, and Jimmy Walker had gotten their starts. It's a club where no one gets paid and where, once a year, owner Budd Friedman will buy you a drink—*maybe*. Now, Tenth Avenue and Forty-fourth Street, where the club is located, is a pretty tough neighborhood late at night. Nick and Marvin Braverman, another comedian who had worked that night, were leaving the club when they were jumped by three Puerto Ricans with knives. Marvin, who unhesitatingly admits to being a coward, went at once for his own wallet. He was just pulling off his jewelry for extra insurance when he heard Nick whisper, "W-w-w-wait, M-m-m-marv—I think w-w-w-we can t-t-take them." Marvin was stunned; he didn't even think about the money, he didn't think about the jewelry, and he didn't think about the Puerto Ricans—all he cared about was getting back inside the Improvisation to repeat this insane story of what Nick Arnold had just said.

Nick likes to drink—better yet, he likes to go drinking with other people, because he claims that's the only time when he can watch everybody else walk like he does. He normally carries around a pocketful of drinking straws in case anyone offers to buy, because he can't drink from a glass. After leaving the show to return back East, Nick decided he wanted to leave California with a bang. For weeks, he had collected empty bourbon bottles in his room on the seventh floor of a Sunset Strip hotel. On his last night in town, he started drinking and, getting progressively morose, began to throw his saved-up bottles out the window—I mean, *cases* of empty bottles. The sidewalk, by late night, was literally blanketed with broken glass —it looked like some mammoth greenhouse had fallen out of the sky. But the Los Angeles mentality being what it is—which is, if possible, even more detached than the New York mentality—no one even bothered to call the police. By the end of the night, Nick was good and angry at the apathy of the people in Los Angeles—so he decided to throw all his furniture out of the window to see if *that* would shake anybody up. This he did, and then passed out on the floor.

In the morning, his car arrived, as planned, to take him to the airport. The crowning blow was that not even the driver was impressed enough to comment— he just steered wordlessly, picking his way down the street. When Nick realized that no one, not even the hotel, had been bothered enough to take steps to have his prize mess cleaned up, he was practically suicidal.

One of Nick's problems, of course, is the fact that he is initially difficult to understand until you get into the rhythm of his speech. He was one of the writers who'd get crazy if he'd written a joke which he thought was particularly funny and Johnny kept rejecting it. He once got so ticked at Johnny that he had a joke mimeographed and submitted it every day for a month. Johnny never did accept it, either.

Like most writers who work on the side on screenplays and also do material for other comics in the business, Nick would occasionally sell material when he needed some bread. There is a classic story involving Nick and Joey Bishop. Nick really hopes that someday he'll be allowed to perform on "The Tonight Show." The possibility of that is pretty remote because of the difficulty in understanding him, and because the palsy is prominent, and because you and I *might* feel uncomfortable. But Nick performs, nonetheless, at

places like the Comedy Store and the Improvisation—
and at those places he's not only encouraged, but he's
a big asset. He was at the Comedy Store doing material
of his own one night—a television announcement in
which Charlton Heston is trying to raise funds for his
favorite charity. Nick decided that Charlton Heston's
favorite charity was diarrhea. Well, Joey Bishop happened to be sitting there that night in the audience,
and, knowing Nick from "The Tonight Show," contacted him about buying that piece of material for
Joey's act in Las Vegas. Nick had worked with Joey on
"The Tonight Show," of course, and he wanted to be
diplomatic, so he said to Joey, "Take it—it's yours. I
give it to you." But Joey insisted on buying it and they
ultimately agreed on a price of $500 (a token payment
at best).

A few weeks later, Joey called Nick and said, "Nick,
I don't understand. When I heard you do this piece of
material it took about five minutes, but when I do it, it
lasts for only about a minute and a half."

Nick replied, "O-o-of c-c-course it d-d-does, you
d-d-dumb s-s-son-of-a-b-b-bitch!"

With that, Joey burst out laughing and Nick agreed
to make up the other three and a half minutes with
additional material he wrote just for Joey.

In 1971, the last year before "The Tonight Show"
moved to its new permanent home in Burbank, California, the show made four trips West. On one of
these West Coast originations, two extra writers were
put on the show. They were Mickey Rose (who seemed
to write jokes only about chickens), and Jeffrey Barron, who was hired based on a strong recommendation
from Mickey. Jeff was never introduced to Johnny, so
when he saw him driving down the hall at NBC with
Fred de Cordova one afternoon, he went over and
said, "Hi, Johnny."

Fred quickly introduced him. "Johnny, this is Jeff
Barron, who will be writing sketches for us while we're
in California."

"I know. He's a good writer. Nice to meet you."

Fred pressed down the pedal of his electric golf cart and sped off. "We've got to be going."

Later Fred came to Jeff and told him to never say "Hello" to Johnny in the hall because it broke Johnny's concentration. Fred kept him well isolated from the staff whenever he could.

One morning Hank Bradford announced that Johnny wanted to see all the writers in his office at 2:00 that afternoon, a summons with distinctly somber overtones. At 2:00 exactly, they paraded into Johnny's office and were joined by Fred.

"Hi, guys. Anyone want any coffee?" Carson offered.

And all the veteran writers shook their heads negatively, as if they knew they shouldn't ever say "yes."

Johnny began the meeting. "I can't do this filth."

Fred jumped in: "No, Johnny doesn't do filth."

Hank asked, "Any of the filth we've submitted in particular?"

"Yes, these three sketches about the sexual revolution."

Jeff had written all three parts of the sketch, but Johnny fortunately didn't know that. One sketch segment involved a judge who was caught hiding in the bushes outside a grade school wearing nothing but a raincoat. But the one that really bugged Johnny went like this:

> OPENING SHOT: Johnny Carson dressed in a white doctor's jacket is standing in his doorway saying good-bye to a sexy young lady.

SEXY YOUNG LADY: Oh, Doctor, thank you so much! I've just never known anyone who's so loving, who's so considerate, and who hugs and kisses and touches so much! [This was during the time when a lot of psychiatrists were getting heavy criticism for sleeping with their patients under the guise of therapy.]

JOHNNY CARSON: Well, it's a new kind of treatment. I like to get as close to my patients as possible.

> CAMERA PULLS BACK TO REVEAL A SIGN NEXT TO THE DOORWAY THAT READS:

DR. CARSON—VETERINARIAN

SEXY YOUNG LADY: We'll be back to see you for sure. You're just so sensitive and affectionate!

JOHNNY CARSON: I look forward to that, my dear.

> CAMERA PULLS BACK FARTHER AND REVEALS THAT THE SEXY YOUNG LADY HAS A CHICKEN ON A LEASH.

BLACK-OUT.

Carson continued the meeting: "I don't fuck chickens!"

Fred added, "Mr. Carson doesn't fuck chickens!"

Carson went on: "I don't do that sort of thing, I never have, and I don't ever want another sketch that suggests I do fuck chickens!"

Hank Bradford, in an attempt to lighten the mood of the meeting, suggested, "Perhaps we could change the chicken to a beaver." At which point Carson threw the scripts at the writers and they paraded out with their egos between their legs. Jeff was grateful at that point that he was only a part-time employee.

Later they found out that Johnny had dinner with Jack Benny the night before, and Jack had repeatedly said, "Johnny, why do you do all that dirty material? You don't need it; you're too good." (Here's a perfect example of Carson responding to the advice of the last person to get his ear.) Three nights later Johnny was doing a piece of special material at the desk after the monologue which was dying. The sixth joke was notably sexual in content, and when Johnny delivered it, he not only got laughs—he got applause. So he glanced over at the writers and said, "I call a big meeting to complain about dirty material, and then I find out that's what the audience wants. Well, guys, back to the filth. . . ."

Life in the Trenches

—What would you like to talk to Johnny
about?
—Have him ask me anything.
(Translation: I am a typical Hollywood
actor so I have never had an original
thought and I have nothing to say of any
interest to anyone anywhere.)

—Talent coordinator to scheduled guest

The fourth unit of the show—after Johnny, the producers and the writers—consists of talent coordinators,
like I had been. The job is to scout, develop, book,
cajole, preinterview and prepare guests for the show. In
terms of temperament, talent coordinators are what you
might call out-patients of the ward. That's owed to the
fact that, theoretically, the job requires extensive contact with all kinds of people out in the real world. Unfortunately, the artists, managers, agents and publicists
with whom we most had to deal could not by any
stretch of the imagination be considered "real."

The life of a coordinator, I think, is best summed up
with the anecdotes from the files of Shirley Wood, who,
of all the members of "The Tonight Show" production
staff, is the one with the most seniority (and, not

coincidentally, the most hard-bitten outlook). Shirley was a coordinator in the difficult days of the change-over from a series of guest hosts to a new regular—"that Carson kid." The show was a shambles then—nobody knew about Johnny Carson or had a clue as to how he'd hold up, so guests were perpetually dropping out of the lineup at the last minute. During that period, Shirley coined a question which has since risen to the top of the charts in the coordinators' top 40. "Who," she wailed, "do you have to fuck to get *out* of show business?"

Several years ago, *Cosmopolitan* magazine did a feature on career women in broadcasting, and one of the people they chose to spotlight was Shirley Wood. Shirley went through the history of how she got the job, talked about what fun it was, and so on, and at one point, the interviewer asked her, "Do you ever date any of the actors who appear on the show?"

Shirley replied, "No, I try never to do that." And then, as a private joke, she whispered to this seemingly friendly woman, "Between you and me, I find they're just terrible in bed."

Well, naturally, that quote wound up in print—in boldface, as I recall—and Shirley was enraged. She was screaming about a lawsuit and saying, "That girl told me she wouldn't print that!"

Peter Lassally asked her, "Shirley, why are you so upset?"

Shirley shouted, "Well, my family reads a lot, and I'm sure someone will see *Cosmo*—can you imagine their reaction if they see that quote of mine in print?"

Peter looked at her with an absolutely straight face and said, "Oh—are some of your relatives actors?"

There is not always a lot of dignity attached to being a coordinator.

For about a year three of the men on "The Tonight Show" became extremely close friends—John Gilroy, the associate producer, Mike Zannella, who was head talent coordinator then, and Bob Garland, the newest of the talent coordinators. The three of them functioned like a sub-plot for the show because they were constantly contriving ways to embarrass and humiliate each other, which they could normally manage to do without each other's help. Mike was going through his hypochondriac stage and carried a briefcase full of medication; Bob lived in the Chelsea Hotel and wore two-dollar sneakers and no socks, regardless of the New York weather; and John liked to have a few drinks and start fires in men's rooms.

Following a taping one night, John and Mike asked Bob to join them for dinner, but he begged off, saying he had no money, but they insisted and said he could pay them back later. They went for dinner at Max's Kansas City, a place where Bob was well known. Max's was the cuisine capital of the Manhattan cultural underground. Toward the end of the meal Bob got a bad case of the hiccups. Normally very shy, Bob became progressively more embarrassed, and Mike and John pretended he was embarrassing them, as well. Finally, John summoned the waiter and asked for a grocery bag. The waiter brought one from the kitchen and Bob began to grow even more suspicious when John told him he could cure his hiccups. They ultimately convinced the gullible Bob Garland to put the bag over his head, pinch it closed around his neck, and then breathe in and out. They assured him his hiccups would be gone on the thirtieth exhale. So Bob, red in the face from all the people at adjoining tables staring at him, complied and began counting out loud inside the bag. When he got to 30, he took the bag off and found he was all alone at the table with a room full of people watching and the check in front of him.

Bob had his revenge by later leaving the show and concentrating on screenwriting. His most notable success was the script he wrote for Jane Fonda and Robert Redford entitled "The Electric Horseman."

Thanks to Rowan and Martin, "beautiful downtown Burbank," home of NBC and "The Tonight Show," will live forever in infamy. If they seemed to always paint Burbank as a flat, ugly, hot, smoggy aesthetic desert, they were merely being kind. Burbank's only redeeming feature, as far as I can see, is that land was cheap—that and the fact that, because the town is devoid of safe (let alone good) restaurants and is walled in by Forest Lawn Cemetery on one side and a dry riverbed on the other, the NBC work force has no place to go but to their offices for the full run of the working day.

Within the rambling NBC complex, the offices of "The Tonight Show" seem to mirror almost religiously the dreary atmosphere of life outside, in Burbank. In New York, "The Tonight Show" offices had been a series of cubicles along an L-shaped hallway on the seventh floor, and had been quite satisfactory. When word had gone out that the show was thinking of moving to L.A., there had been a flurry of high-flown pronouncements from NBC indicating that Oz-like quarters beyond our wildest dreams were awaiting us. Such grandiosity was in the air that even the Hollywood trade papers bubbled with the news of this palatial "high-rise." It was a fine piece of P.R., and out West we came. What, in fact, awaited us was a hideous structure of bolted-together, pre-fab modular boxes reminiscent of flat Quonset huts—a comparison exaggerated even further by the generous coat of military green paint that covered it both inside and out. Worse still, the thermostats were modular, so adjoining sections of the building varied radically in temperature, depending on whether they were in the shade or in the sun. The temperature stayed at either 61 or 89, with no middle ground, and as a result the complex came to be regarded as an experimental breeding ground for new strains of influenza.

Into this psychic battleground, every day by 11 A.M., walked the intrepid production staff.

Usually, the first person to hit the bungalow—at about 10 A.M.—was Fred de Cordova. Fred felt he needed this extra time to catch up on gossip with the cleaning lady and to compile, refine, and revise his lists, which were legion. I tended to wander in at about 10:45, and after looking over my fascinating mail (which usually consisted of bulk fliers and hackneyed press releases), I'd plop down in Fred's office with a sharp pencil and a cup of tea to wait for the others. Eventually, they'd trickle in—all but Shirley Wood. Inevitably five, ten, or fifteen minutes later, Shirley would charge in, gushing about the construction on her street, or about her sprinklers that wouldn't shut off, or about having to take her dog to the vet, or about the overnight power failure that had made all her clocks run late. We used to look forward, with some annoyance, to each of Shirley's new and creative alibis. Occasionally, we'd remind her that this made two power failures and three construction jobs in the same two-week period, but Shirley didn't waver.

Once settled, we'd all turn to the five-by-fifteen-foot cork booking board on Fred's office wall. This is the scaffolding on which egos, clout, and politics are shuffled around until it's been determined which four or five public personalities wanting to say something in front of 15,000,000 people will be given the chance on which particular night. The board is covered with three-by-five cards, arranged in rows by date for about eight week's worth of shows, and each card represents a particular star. There was a variety of cryptic symbols on each of the cards, indicating the stage of completion each individual booking had reached—but there was one in particular that always made trouble. It was the final mark awaited on each card—the "green check." Green-checking, a term coined on "The Tonight Show," is merely a euphemism for a blacklisting system, and as with most such systems, it richly deserves to be exposed. It works like this: each day, the head coordinator's assistant made a list of the new prospective guests and sent it to Joe Cuniff, the show's liaison, who then turned it over to David Tebet, a man who claimed some cockamamie title like "vice president of talent," and who, to everyone's chagrin, believed himself to be in full charge of "The Tonight Show." In truth, his job was to keep NBC executives and celebrities happy, a responsibility he discharged mainly by giving away color television sets like some people drop business cards. (Some people have actually gotten 3 or 4 of these sets, a privilege which must present some kind of storage problem for them. Johnny once said he knows that at his grave, in the middle of his funeral, everything will suddenly stop and a color television set will arrive from Dave Tebet.)

So, Dave and Joe look over the list of names, and then they'd pull a few out and call the coordinators to say, "Why her?", or, "Why him?" If the answer was not to their satisfaction, the guest would not get the green "go-ahead" check and could not do the show. Of course, there are other people who have veto power—Johnny and NBC executives, to name a few—but most of the green-checking got done by Dave and Joe. Not surprisingly, there was a strong tendency to approve of NBC contract stars and to disapprove of everybody else, although in total contradiction, there was a period of time they used to refuse to allow us to use RCA recording artists, or authors from Random House, which they also owned. There are plenty of examples of rotten green-checking in my memory.

We once had on the show a sensational guest—and a wonderful man—by the name of Robert Townsend. He had been president of everything from American Express to Avis, and he epitomized the successful, inventive business executive. He had written a slim, very hip little book called *Up the Organization,* in which a lot of seemingly radical but also very sensible ideas were put forth. For example, in one of his businesses— I believe it was Avis—he had refused to allow any of his executives to have personal secretaries. That meant that all their typing had to be done by typing pools and so on, but mainly, it forced them to place and answer their own phone calls, and it meant that a secretary was protected from picking up the man's dry-cleaning and watering his plants. He also felt that when someone was concerned enough to call and fight his way through to talk to the president of Avis, then the president of Avis ought to be concerned enough to pick up the phone. Townsend also believed that the nicest offices in the building should be occupied not by the top executives, but by the people who had the most frequent contact with the public and who therefore had much to do with first impressions of the company: the receptionists. If you want happy telephone receptionists, Townsend reasoned, you don't stick them away in a windowless basement with uncomfortable furniture.

I had arranged for Townsend to do the show, and I routinely submitted his name for a green check. The ensuing hassle was literally unbelievable. The reasoning went that here was a man who had been president of Avis, and who would therefore presumably discuss on the show his career with that company—but shortly before that the parent company of NBC, which was RCA, had purchased Hertz. The powers that were did not want Avis, the competition, getting any free air time on their network. So, a debate raged back and forth and finally it was agreed that Townsend could discuss Avis, but he couldn't say anything derogatory about Hertz. Now, already that looks like some sort of conflict between self-interest and ethical broadcasting standards, but, okay—Townsend understood and laughingly agreed. However, during the course of the on-air interview, Johnny brought up the question of nepotism in big business. Townsend discussed several firms, singling out Ford Motor Company as having suffered the most in product quality by not relinquishing family control—but, Townsend went on, the worst case of nepotism he'd *ever* seen was the dynastic reign of the Sarnoffs at NBC. Needless to say, the repercussions of that statement were staggering, and the decision came down that Townsend was to be forever barred from doing *any* show on the NBC network.

The blacklisting of Ralph Nader took place under similar circumstances. When I went to get Nader green-checked, I again found that there was a problem. The "problem," of course, was that Ralph Nader is not squeamish about whom he attacks—and one of the things he had initially attacked was the Corvair, a General Motors car. He had actually caused the discontinuation of the entire Corvair line. When General Motors saw what he had done, they put the screws to their advertising outlets—including NBC—and informed them, I'm told, that anyone giving Ralph Nader more than essential hard-news publicity would no longer be enjoying G.M. advertising dollars. If the fact that NBC buckled under to this kind of threat does not violate the letter of the law, it certainly violates the morality and ethics of honest public broadcasting.

The only time that green-checking ever got amusing for the staff was when it came face to face with ratings wars. During periods known in the industry as "ratings sweeps," there would arise a special kind of conflict between the NBC programming people, the staff of "The Tonight Show," and the NBC hierarchy (i.e., Dave Tebet). If it was found that ratings for the show had slid a little, the programming people would scream, "Big Names! We need more Big Names on this show!"

So, all right, we'd hunt around and ask, "Who's a Big Name?" And maybe we'd check the top TV shows and come up with, say, Carroll O'Connor. We'd contact Carroll and make the arrangements, and suddenly we'd find that we couldn't get a *green check* for Carroll O'Connor. Why? Because Carroll was on a CBS show that was beating hell out of the opposite programming on NBC, and the reasoning went that NBC shouldn't offer to publicize the star of a show that was already costing them a lot of ratings points. So much, then, for more Big Names during rating weeks.

In any case, once the green check was on, the name of a talent coordinator would appear on the corner of the guest's three-by-five card. I am ashamed to admit that much of the morning meeting would be given over to arguments about these guest assignments, but that ritual also produced 60 minutes of some of the most concentrated, funny hostility I've ever been party to. Examining a potential guest was an exercise in arrogance; nothing and no one was sacred. I remember one case in which a coordinator was wondering how to handle Little Stevie Wonder, who was at the time in the interim period between his childhood career and his current superstardom. Rudy Tellez stopped the meeting and said, "How are we supposed to get this blind kid to come out and hit his mark to do the song?"

The producer, Stan Irvin, thought a minute, then said, "I've got it. We'll use a set that looks like a ship deck, put Stevie in a sailor's suit, and have him walk out holding onto the railing." It was like that every day.

There was a lot of conflict over the dividing up of guests. The guests fell basically into three categories: there were those who were gregarious, easy to get along with, and made for a good show (a coordinator's dream); there were those who were considerate and nice, but who basically had nothing to say (and would therefore burn up half a day in pre-interviews); and there were those who were just plain uncooperative and rude. The latter are usually people who believe themselves to be of major significance. Some are notorious for breaking appointments—as many as three or four for one appearance. If you need a minimum of 30 minutes to get prepared for a show, some will give you three, and then demand their own hairdresser or makeup man during the precious last minutes. So, the coordinators were constantly fighting among themselves to keep the guests they had or to foist the ones they didn't want onto somebody else. So much, then, for the morning meeting.

Lunch was a thing that talent coordinators rarely had time for, since the period between 12:15 and taping time was the period of heaviest activity for them. New guests had to be pre-interviewed—that is, coached—in person. "Regular" guests had to be phoned and primed with ideas. Then, a frantic series of telephone calls and writing would ensue before the bells of 3:30 struck, because that's the hour when Fred would start annoyingly roaming the halls bellowing "Notes! Notes!" for his final meeting with Johnny.

These were also the hours given to the continuing pursuit of the elusive Big Name personalities, and the hours of trying to find new ways to politely say "no" to those personalities who had run out of steam or who were simply not suitable for the show. Sometimes there were also tapes of prospective guests to watch, an activity which is the modern equivalent of talent auditions.

In the midst of all this, you might have to drop everything and go over to make sure the guests got there. Then you had to find out how much of their music they'd left behind and send someone to fetch it, or call wardrobe and say, "Can you have this pressed?", or, "Can you sew a sleeve back on this dress?" Then the act's rehearsal would invariably point up some dissonance or poor arranging that would have to be reworked by Doc, and that meant more time and rehearsing.

At around 4:15 the band takes a break, and at 4:30 there is a final production meeting in which the show is run down for everyone's benefit. Theoretically, at that point everyone knows everything there is to know about what the show will look like. Then, many rude remarks are exchanged about the shoddy jobs everyone has done, and the bodies wander off on their own ways. What follows is, surprisingly, the most relaxing part of the day, because by that time nothing much can be done, pro or con, to alter what's to come.

Fred wanders around, poking his head in and out of cubicles, and then strips to the waist, slaps on a quart and a half of some highly aggressive cologne, and changes to look dressier for the show.

The talent coordinators usually put their feet up, make a few more phone calls, and try to relax. At about 5:00, the guests begin to arrive and the coordinators either wait anxiously for the late ones or take the ones who've arrived to their dressing rooms, where they go over the guests' previously discussed material, show them into makeup, and make sure the stage manager knows where to find them when their segment approaches.

Around this time, Ed is ready to go out onstage to warm up the audience, which had begun queueing up about two hours before. At 18 minutes after the hour, the band trudges across the stage and each member takes his seat. What begins at that moment is a period of concentrated theatrical pressure (*i.e.,* hype) on the audience so that they will feel lively, excited about the show, and part of the behind-the-scenes "magic." After a few minutes, Fred de Cordova comes striding across the stage looking gallant and sleek and says a few words to the band, which in turn plays a few bars to him. Fred then goes to the microphone sitting on a stand before the audience, explains who he is, tells them how delighted he is that they could come, and in turn introduces Doc Severinsen. Doc appears to a fanfare from the band and, always dressed outrageously, takes a bow of Elizabethan flourish, which the audience loves. Then he greets the band and strikes up the music. After about a minute and a half, the tune ends, the audience applauds, and Doc takes the microphone. He announces that the audience has now witnessed the entire rehearsal of "The Tonight Show" at no extra charge, and then he, in turn, introduces Ed again. Ed comes out and speaks to the audience for three or four minutes, reminding them to look their best since they may be on camera, telling them where to look for their cues, making sure that the applause sign is working, and explaining that it will keep them as spontaneous as possible. He also gives a little pitch which in essence says that "The Tonight Show" is indeed a comedy show, so the audience should by all means have no reservations about laughing as long and as loud as they like. He gets his time cues from the stage manager, and as it gets down to a minute before tape time, the anticipation is high. Every night is, in its own way, like opening night. Johnny is pacing backstage alone, and then—at exactly 5:30—the show begins.

It also ends—to everyone's relief—exactly 87½ minutes later. I think that most people and a lot of first-time performers are sure that when the show is over, the cast and staff go running off to the Brown Derby or someplace terribly exciting for a big party. That's hardly the case. Everyone says thank you and good night. Johnny goes up to his dressing room, gets out of his makeup, and carries on a post-mortem of the show with Peter, Fred, and Bobby Quinn in which he invariably details some displeasure. He always has at least one negative comment to make, and he often spends the meeting talking about how he never wants to see so-and-so back on the show again—a decree that may hold up for six minutes or six years.

The talent coordinators tell their guests how sensational they were, and then go and collect their things, throw them in the car, and split. It's simply another working day. Often, at least two or three nights a week, I would get myself organized, grab a hamburger, and try to see a screening of a film or a new performer at a club before wandering home, sometimes as late as 2:00 in the morning. A few of the stagehands and a few of the writers will probably wander across the street and have a drink before heading to either Orange County or Woodland Hills, and then the day is officially over.

Tiptoe Through
the Tulips

They don't take any chances at "The Tonight Show," no sir. The show is as tight as a rock. You have to go up there and talk to those what-you-may-call-its, those talent coordinators. The show has no spontaneity. Everyone is scared of making a mistake.

—Unnamed guest

I've been asked the question many times: "How does someone get to be a talent coordinator on 'The Tonight Show,' and what qualifications do you have to have?"

The answer is: "It depends."

In my case, it was through having a varied career background which had given me at least some experience in a lot of different areas of show business. I had a degree in dramatic literature (totally useless), I had done various kinds of free-lance television writing, written comic books, worked as a newspaper stringer, been an agent, a stage manager, a gofer, and then for two and a half years prior to "The Tonight Show," I had directed the Television Departments for two public relations firms. At the time, probably my strongest recommendation for the job was that I was available on a week's notice.

Bob Dolce was a graphic artist for "The Today Show" and did volunteer work with the guests on a telethon with Rudy Tellez, making his transition to "The Tonight Show" that way. Today he's the best. Others were talent coordinators on local talk shows, which seems to be the most common method of advancement.

Perhaps the most challenging—and risky—responsibility of a talent coordinator is the searching out of new long-term guest prospects for the show. For years, people have criticized "The Tonight Show" for using the same guests over and over—they are convinced that there are thousands of brilliant and witty people out here, including their favorite star, who would be perfect on the show. They're wrong. A lot of correspondence also comes in from civilians—people with no particular credentials or talents—who say, "Why don't you have me on? I'm no one—wouldn't that be an interesting change?" Wrong again. The fact is, the same guests have to be used over and over—for a couple of good reasons.

One, they have to fit Johnny's definition of the word "entertaining." Now, "entertaining" can be a difficult concept to keep a grip on, since everybody's idea of what it is varies depending on what they ate the night before—but the basics are even more difficult to grasp when Johnny's ideas of them are constantly changing at the same time. His inconsistency is not caused so much by what he ate for dinner, but by what he didn't get served up on last night's show, and there was always something he felt was missing.

So elusive was this concept of "entertaining" that a regular meeting was held once a month to review the definition. In this meeting, which constituted the coordinators' only formalized, direct contact with Carson, he would advise us on the new guidelines for "entertaining" and the new list of guests who had ceased to *be* "entertaining"—and we would repeat our

JOHNNY TONIGHT!

Suntanned and relaxed, Johnny and Joanna Carson vacation on the French Riviera. Johnny prefers to holiday where he is not apt to be recognized, a rare and admirable characteristic since many Hollywood stars get insecure when they're someplace where they're not important. *(Credit: Peter C. Borsari)*

Johnny and Ed McMahon, posing with childhood pictures. Apparently the sailor suits had their effect for later Johnny served as a naval officer in World War II, while Ed became a Marine Corps fighter pilot.

(Credit: Nate Cutler/Globe Photos)

Here's an older photograph from Johnny's earlier days on "The Tonight Show." Note the hair color, the narrow necktie and the vintage microphone. Also, Johnny is rarely caught smoking on camera anymore. He does, however, sneak a puff periodically from a cigarette hidden in an ashtray under his desk. *(Credit: United Press International)*

Muhammad Ali has been a regular and popular guest on "The Tonight Show" for many years. This photograph was taken in New York City and reveals that only Carson has retained his fighting weight. It might appear as if Ed McMahon has lost interest, but that's not the case. Ed is looking off at a television monitor knowing that the camera is not on him.

(Credit: Alpha Blair/Pictorial Parade)

Ed McMahon plays straight man to Carson's Aunt Blabby during a charity benefit performance. Do you suppose Ed still owns this leisure suit? *(Credit: Peter C. Borsari)*

Robin Williams and Johnny. This is a fascinating photograph because it shows the obvious affinity between Johnny and Robin, although Robin has never been a guest on "The Tonight Show." Robin's manager has purposely kept Robin off talk shows to keep him from being overexposed. "The Dick Cavett Show" is the only exception and that's explainable since Robin's manager also handles Cavett.

(Credit: Peter C. Borsari)

Johnny rarely gets on a bandwagon, although he will occasionally start one. After Bert Parks was fired as host of The Miss America Pageant, Johnny asked his audience to support a drive to reinstate Parks. The next day's mail included this T-shirt and button showing the public was ready to get involved. *(Credit: Wide World Photos)*

Carson, who normally shies away from awards, did however go back to Cambridge, Massachusetts in 1977 to receive the Hasty Pudding Pot, emblematic of Harvard University's Hasty Pudding Club 11th Annual Man of the Year, following such men as Jack Lemmon, Robert Redford, Paul Newman and Bob Hope. *(Credit: United Press International)*

Ed McMahon got married for the second time on March 6, 1976. This made it easy for him to remember his anniversary since it was also his 52nd birthday. Ed's bride was Victoria Valentine of Houston, Texas.

(Credit: United Press International)

An early publicity still of Carl "Doc" Severinsen.
(Credit: United Press International)

When he later took over "The Tonight Show" orchestra, his stature, hair and wardrobe grew proportionately.

(Credit: Wide World Photos)

For years Doc's wardrobe was expected to change and get wilder and more absurd with every show. Here, posed with his daughter Nancy, he's wearing a sweater and pants outfit in a strawberry motif. One Valentine's Day, Carson stunned the censors by noting during the monologue that Doc's sweater was certainly in keeping with the holiday. He said to Doc, "I notice you have a heart-on."

(Credit: United Press International)

"The Tonight Show" helped lift many performers into nationwide prominence—Mac Davis among many others. Doc once mentioned to Mac that he'd thought of a great lyric line for a song. Mac took the one line and turned it into a huge hit; the residuals he generously shared with Doc. The line Doc gave him was also the title of the song: "Stop and Smell the Roses."
(Credit: Frank Edwards Fotos International)

Johnny and his brother Dick attend a costume party with a western theme. Dick Carson left his directing job at "The Tonight Show" in New York to direct the prime-time "Don Rickles Show." When it was canceled, Dick went on to direct the rival "Merv Griffin Show." The woman behind them is Doc's ex-wife, Yvonne. *(Credit: Peter C. Borsari)*

Denim and bandannas are both work and party wear in Hollywood. In this particular instance, the Carsons are dancing at the annual SHARE party, a chic invitation-only charity ball. Johnny is usually the emcee. Joanna is also deeply involved as both a performer and an organizer. Much of the entertainment is done by the wives of the celebrities. (Note the design in Joanna's blouse.) (*Credit: Peter C. Borsari*)

Carson has contemplated leaving "The Tonight Show" for years, but on May 2, 1979, he told the viewing audience that he intended to stay through 1979 and possibly through most of 1980, and maybe even complete his full two-year contract with NBC. Johnny is holding a fragment of guest Raquel Welch's dress, which he recovered after an Academy Award broadcast. *(Credit: United Press International)*

Johnny and NBC Network President Fred Silverman smile amicably for the camera, although for months they had been unable to reach any agreement in contract negotiations, as illustrated by the bottom photograph. *(Credit: Globe Photos)*

On May 6, 1980 NBC announced that Carson would continue on "The Tonight Show" for three more years, working an increased 4 nights a week—however, in a reduced 60 minute format. Carson's NBC salary remains the same—in the 3–5 million dollar category—which is reputed to be approximately ⅓ of his yearly gross income. The rest is generated by personal appearances, investments and his apparel company.

(Credit: United Press International)

Johnny mops up after a previous act has left the stage a mess. As always, Johnny Carson has the last laugh.

(Credit: Peter C. Borsari)

time-worn lament about this endless narrowing of our field of choices. Johnny often emphasized, as he closed the meeting, that he never wanted to completely rule out any category or type of guest, or even any particular subject matter. Anything went, he would say, as long as it was interesting and not in hopelessly bad taste. Although that was his official line, it was not the whole truth about what made a guest acceptable to Johnny.

There was another quality equal in importance to "entertaining," and that quality—when it was referred to out loud—was known as "rapport." Now, "rapport" is, if anything, even more elusive than "entertaining," but the backbone of its meaning has to do with a guest's ability to complement Johnny's performance. In other words, those guests with the most rapport are also those who know whose show it is. If they can make Johnny feel at home, if they can set up some good one-liners for him, they have rapport. If they aren't totally unpredictable or aggressive—that is, if they don't try to take over the show—then they have rapport. To be long-winded, or highbrow, or political —or, God forbid, abstract—is to definitely *not* have rapport. Where that leaves a coordinator who wants to remain a coordinator is with the task of finding brilliant and time-tested performers with a taste for humble pie. If there ever was such a species, it has left a limited trace on this planet and is one of many endangered species.

The second problem is that there aren't too many artists with that special blend of qualities that makes them amusing in an open format like "Tonight." Ironically, most performers are either limited in intellectual scope and are therefore dull, or they're unable to really *talk*—that is, converse outside of a role. Moss Hart said in his wonderful book, *Act I,* that "the theater is the inevitable refuge of the unhappy child." People who go into performing seem to be seeking recognition—or a degree of it—that they feel they can't get from their families or peer groups. With the audience, the relationship has a slightly removed, unreal quality that makes it easier for insecure people to seem gregarious. Not so, though, on a talk show. When they are forced to extemporize, to be themselves on a one-to-one basis, these larger-than-life people tend to be shy or even inarticulate. What's more, on a talk show there is no script, per se—just notes about a general direction to aim in—and for someone who's used to hiding in full character, that can be terrifying. I saw that insecurity at its most extreme in the case of actress Greer Garson. She and her husband at one time owned Ack Ack, the 1971 Racehorse of the Year—and Greer came on the show to talk about him. As she and Johnny sat and chatted, he would interrupt her periodically and ask a question about the animal, and every time he did, she would shoot him a confused look and then go right on as if he hadn't spoken. I can remember walking backstage as this interview was deteriorating into a monologue by Miss Garson and seeing Mike Zannella, her coordinator, staring with a frozen look on his face. He was holding a crumbled piece of paper she had discarded with the interview she had memorized on it, and was reading her "conversation" off the page, almost word for word. She had actually written her dialogue down in advance like a script; she felt incapable, after so many years of acting, of talking spontaneously, even about her own horse.

Most of the people who both wear well on the show and have "rapport" with Johnny seem to be New York-trained entertainers like Robert Blake, Burt Reynolds, Joan Rivers, and Tony Randall. I've never attributed this to the superior training of New York actors, but more to the environment that forces a person to think on his feet not only to get ahead, but to survive the life-style. In Los Angeles, on the other hand, a person can be "born, grow up, die, and never leave his car." When your entire vocabulary can be limited to "Is the surf up?" and "Two tacos to go," a Los Angelean is about as exciting as smog.

Ironically, those who actually do boast the "biggest names" in films and television are rarely interesting guests. For example, there probably isn't a nicer, more stable man in the business than Clint Eastwood—not to mention the fact that he is also the world's number-one box office attraction—but when out of character on a talk show, the man isn't inspiring. People would certainly tune in to see him, but they wouldn't watch for long—Eastwood is simply too reserved and too private to have the stuff for high-powered "personality" entertainment.

The "thinking" guest, the one with a broad range of personal experiences and unusual convictions, is the only guest of real value to a show like "The Tonight Show," and talent coordinators are forever beating the bushes in hopes of developing just one of them. Even if you find one, the first time is always a gamble. Some coordinators won't even try it—they say, and I quote: "Why should I go out and see new acts or try to find new people? Why should I take a chance with Johnny's precious 'rapport' when I have a mortgage to pay?"

The producer, for example, takes no responsibility for recruiting or developing talent, and yet he is the first to claim credit if a new guest makes a hit. Likewise, he will deny any involvement if the new guest bombs. That attitude could be summed up like this: "It's your neck, kid—unless he makes it." That is not the most inspiring climate in which to take risks. This mentality gets extreme at times—like the time Fred de Cordova registered horror over the fact that I had booked David Brenner. Fred shook his head negatively, saying, "He'll bomb. You'd better watch out." And Fred said something like that right through David's first 30 appearances.

The one time anyone can recall Fred getting involved with developing talent was with Beverly Garland. He kept insisting that Beverly, who had been one of his stars on "My Three Sons," would make a sensational guest for the show. All the talent coordinators kept evading the issue, changing the subject, and running away, because we knew she wouldn't work. Fred wouldn't let up, though, and finally Beverly was booked. This erstwhile charming guest did nothing the entire time but plug the Howard Johnson's Lodge she owned, and she ended up being a screaming bore. So much, then, for the instincts of a producer.

Surprisingly, Johnny realizes that he is a poor judge of prospective talent and he knows better than to get involved in booking decisions—unless it's someone he's sure he *doesn't* want on the show. This laissez-faire policy of his was arrived at partially through a series of bad experiences. Once, when the show was headquartered in New York, Johnny had the notion that he should get more involved in choosing the talent, so he decided to attend an audition. Those were held across the street from 30 Rockefeller Center at the Johnny Victor theater, and they were sessions in which a dozen acts would come on in succession to be judged by the talent staff. On the day Johnny chose to attend, one of the performers was a tall, beautiful blonde who came out very appealingly, focused straight down on Johnny, and started singing "Makin' Whoopee" to him. The problem was, she had rewritten all the verses, substituting every piece of nasty sexual gossip she'd ever heard about Johnny for the regular lyrics. Johnny sat there frozen with a scarlet face for the entire eight minutes of the song, and he never came to an audition again.

Naturally, Johnny meets a lot of entertainers socially, and is constantly being "hit on" for a spot on the show, either by agents, by the performers themselves, and even by the performers' wives. He's great at saying, "Sure you should be on the show—definitely. Listen, I'll look into it—I'll check it out." And then of course he does nothing. He has a talent for skirting the issue, instead of coming right out and saying, "Hey, I don't get involved in that—go through the regular channels."

One deviation I recall was when Johnny saw The

Manhattan Transfer at a local club and really loved them. After the show, their manager, Aaron Russo, came over to Johnny and said, "Jesus, Johnny—we can't get booked on the show. It's crazy."

Johnny said, "Is that right?" And he came back to us saying, "Those guys are great! Why the hell haven't they been on the show?"

I replied, "I love them, but for now they're a club act—they somehow don't work nearly as well on television."

Johnny didn't like the answer, but he wouldn't pursue it, wouldn't risk a confrontation. I knew he was stewing about my response—*and* about the fact that they'd been on other national shows, but not on his. Shortly after that, they were on the "Dinah" show and did not do well under the close inspection of the camera. I also remember hoping fervently that Johnny had seen them do it.

More often than not, sticking your neck out as a coordinator on a new act would pay off—especially if you'd done your homework. For one thing, you learned whose instincts you could trust for referrals and whose you couldn't. If Joan Rivers was the manager of the farm team for comedy writers, Budd Friedman, owner of the Improvisation, was manager of the farm team for new talent on the show. Budd was responsible for bringing me Bette Midler, whose career on "The Tonight Show" was probably the most interesting odyssey of its kind I ever watched. She had done moderately well on Broadway, having had the good fortune to be cast as one of Tevye's daughters in *Fiddler on the Roof*, but she had also been working pretty steadily as a waitress at the Improvisation. Anyway, one day I got a call from Budd (whom I owed many favors), who said, "Listen, I want to bring Bette over for one of the open auditions." I took his word for her "unique quality" and agreed.

Well, Bette showed up at the Johnny Victor in a dress that she called "antique," but which to this day I believe was a Salvation Army reject, the only thing she could afford on her starving artist's budget. In preparing for the show, she had somehow managed to rip the back of the dress all the way up to her butt.

When Budd saw it, he came to me and said, "Do you think she ought to forget about the audition, or shall we just try to fix the dress up and go ahead?"

I said, "Oh, hell, it's so tough to get people into these auditions. Since she's here, do what repair you can and have her go on."

Bette came out and did beautifully, completely unconscious of the dress. Still, it was a bizarre experience, watching her turn around as she got really involved in the song, and seeing the whole back of her dress loosely held together with safety pins. The next day, at the audition post-mortem, everyone agreed that, even if they weren't sure exactly what it was Bette had, she certainly was interesting. So we booked her on the show. Almost immediately, I turned her over to another talent coordinator, Bob Dolce, who I admit has more sensitivity toward and understanding of women than I do, and who helped nurture her through her first dozen appearances on "The Tonight Show" —appearances which have no doubt done more for her career than any other single break. In this era, Bette not only called Bob for career advice, but to ask what she should have for dinner. Typically, in a recent article, in which she chronicled her rise to superstardom, she never mentioned "The Tonight Show." Johnny, to his credit, immediately recognized her ability, and even took her to Las Vegas with him as his opening act. Unfortunately, it was too early—the audience didn't understand her style at all, and Johnny didn't ask her back.

More than referrals, more than guidelines, more than any other single thing, coordinators have to develop *instincts* for sniffing out new talent. Sometimes the instincts are just hunches based only on a line from a magazine article or the title of a book. Sometimes these turn into real "finds"—strange or wonderful people who could last on the show for years, but who might have gone completely unnoticed without a lucky guess. I can remember reading in *Life* magazine some years ago about a unique sex manual called *Everything You Ever Wanted to Know About Sex (But Were Afraid to Ask)*, and I decided to track down the author, one Dr. David Reuben, out in California. He turned out to be one of the few major guests I ever went out on a limb for and booked based *just* on a telephone interview, for there was no way he could get out to New York for a pre-interview, and he sounded too interesting to pass up. Dr. Reuben had an amazing way of handling clinical language—he could overcome all the normal "dirty word" taboos. He could say on television for the first time words like "masturbate" and "penis" and "orgasm" in such a psychologically soothing manner that it somehow did not embarrass the audience—I mean, they didn't even giggle, which was unheard of. He was on the show many times, and through his savvy about what would fascinate the audience, was able to turn his book into one of the biggest non-fiction best sellers of the decade. The moment I remember best with Dr. Reuben occurred during an on-air discussion about, for some reason, masturbation. Sitting next to Dr. Reuben on that show was mad David Steinberg. Dr. Reuben began with the fact that most children start masturbating in some way as early as six months old, but are often scolded and retain guilt about it throughout their entire lives. Before he could go another step, David interrupted and said, "Gee, Doctor, the only reason *I* feel guilty about masturbation is because I do it so badly." That was the only time I remember anyone being able to break down Reuben's clinical spell.

Freddie Prinze, you'll recall, shot himself even though he was surrounded with friends and success. But mostly I remember him also as one of my most rewarding ventures on "The Tonight Show." Although his appearance on the show is credited with kicking off his career, it technically isn't quite true. He had made his first appearance on the revived "Jack Paar Show" several months before. I can remember seeing him doing light emcee chores at the Improvisation in New York as many as seven years before, when he was still a high school student. At that time, he worked almost totally "blue" and was a genuinely unpleasant young man. He begged for laughs and, like some bad Borscht Belt comic, grew filthier and filthier when he didn't get them. I remember being amazed a couple of years later when his manager, Dave Jonas, sent me a videotape cassette of Freddie on Paar's show. It sat on my desk for several weeks until enough tapes collected so I could fill an hour's worth of viewing time, and when I finally got around to looking at it, I *wasn't* expecting to be pleased. I was flabbergasted. Freddie was polished, professional, and very funny. I couldn't wait to book him. The tape was my first exposure to his character Rivera the Janitor, and I think it was the first time a slovenly Puerto Rican character had openly been a part of New York humor, although his spiritual brother had run my building in New York. Even the man running the cassette machine cracked up, and that convinced me that my instincts about this young man were right. In those days, I didn't have to go through a long-winded pitch to try a new act on the show, but I was nervous about Freddie. *Freddie* was nervous about Freddie, too, and I remember him pacing in near-panic backstage before his segment.

When Fred de Cordova spied him, he came over and grabbed me violently by the arm and said, "Is that Prinze?" I said it was, and Fred said, "He's one of the most unattractive kids I've ever seen. I'm not putting him on the show."

I said, "You've got no choice. It's two minutes before tape time."

Fred stood firm. "He's not going on—Johnny will hate him." I let it slide and crossed my fingers. Although Fred tried to work the show so there was no room for Prinze, the first several guests finished quickly, and Fred had no choice but to let Prinze go out. Freddie was sensational—in fact, he got as close to a standing ovation as any young comic has ever received on "The Tonight Show." From there, of course, he went almost immediately on to star in "Chico and the Man."

All the coordinators, the producer, and even Johnny have built-in biases against certain guests or types of guests, and once a bias has been established, a coordinator often has to bully and hound and simply wait out the opposition to get a break for a performer he believes in. I had to do that with McLean Stevenson. I first met McLean early in my "Tonight Show" career. He had made quite a name for himself in commercials, and was recommended to me as being an absolute talk show "natural." When he came into my office, I found him very aggressive and very eager to please, but lacking in substance—the classic profile of people who are billed by laymen as "naturals." I liked him, but I couldn't in all conscience book him on the show. By our second meeting, which I held at the insistence of his manager, Gene Lesser, MacLean was beginning his role as Colonel Blake on "M*A*S*H," and I found him a very entertaining second-banana type, but still not suitable for "The Tonight Show." Gradually, I watched with interest as he polished his style and rose to great popularity on "M*A*S*H," and when I finally scheduled him for a third interview, he came in with a series of wonderfully funny stories. I recommended him immediately for a spot.

McLean had appeared on "The Doris Day Show," which had for a long time been directed by none other than Fred de Cordova, and when I mentioned booking McLean to Fred, he said, "Hey, I directed him on 'The Doris Day Show,' and he never did say anything funny—the only thing he ever said was: 'Why don't I have more funny lines?' The guy just isn't funny, Craig."

I then went into my wear-down tactics, but it took me no less than six months to get the go-ahead. By that time, *McLean* had gotten cold feet, and it took me another six months to re-persuade *him*. Nevertheless, when he finally came on, he of course worked out to be a sensational guest—in fact, I think he was asked to guest-host sooner than any non-superstar who has ever done the show. There's no question that "The Tonight Show" turned McLean's career around—however, the show should not be held responsible for either of McLean's subsequent series, "In the Beginning" or "Hello, Larry."

My most difficult booking, the one that took the longest to finally see through, was Bruce Dern's. Bruce, when I first met him, was a highly employable character actor; the only catch was that he was working almost exclusively as a psychotic. I remember him telling me that he had fled New York, where he had been extraordinarily successful in Tennessee Williams plays, straight into a job for Alfred Hitchcock in which he played a demented migrant laborer whose avocation was eating babies. He was nominated for an Emmy from that one performance, and was unfortunately typecast as a creep for many years afterward. He worked regularly, but it wasn't the work he wanted to do. It took me months to get him booked, and even when he was pre-interviewed, rehearsed, and squared away, we all had the strange feeling that there was no telling just what Bruce might say or do out there. Bruce, though he is as gentle a man as I know, gives off the distinct aura of an axe murderer. No question about it. The first time he came to my office as a semi-unknown, he managed to cause mild mayhem on the lot. I can remember having appointments with half a dozen people that day, some of them totally bizarre, and all of them managed to get through the guard gate without the least bit of trouble. But Bruce, although he was better dressed that day than I've seen him on many occasions (and on many appearances on "The Tonight Show"), showed up at the gate and the guards just hit the brakes. They called me three different times to make sure that I wanted this man to pass through. Bruce has a pair of cold, cold eyes, and the unpredictable violence he unwittingly projects did not sit well with the guards. When he came in, we talked pleasantly, we discussed running—which we were both interested in, although his success at it is vastly greater than mine—and I then spent a total of 18 months trying to get the go-ahead to book him. I think it was a matter of bull-headed perseverance more than anything else. It's been a while now since he's done the show, which I think is a shame. Bruce is potentially as fine a talk-show guest as Robert Blake or Burt Reynolds or Suzanne Pleshette, but I believe he is trying at this point to keep a low profile, á la Steve McQueen and Robert Redford, and I have to admire him for it.

The greatest risk I ever took, but the one that also did most to project a forward-looking image onto my career, was the booking of Tiny Tim. First of all, I was young for the job when I was hired as a coordinator, and my judgment was constantly being tested by the skeptical production staff. One afternoon I got a call from Sandy Gallin, a theatrical manager who had at one time been my boss at the General Artists Corporation. He told me that he had just taken on a client—a novelty performer by the name of Tiny Tim —who had already made two *major* television appearances and was perfect for the show. These major appearances turned out to be a fifteen-second throwaway shot on the "Laugh-In" series, and a dismal appearance on "The Merv Griffin Show," where Merv, unfortunately, had treated him like a freak. Tiny was always a sympathetic character, and to Merv's surprise, the audience wound up being on Tiny's side and resenting Merv's snide asides. In fact, at the end of Tiny's spot, Merv jokingly asked the audience if they wanted Tiny Tim back, and to his surprise, they yelled, *"Yes!"* But Tiny has an intricate sense of right and wrong and he had firmly declined that show's subsequent offers, preferring to disappear back into the anonymity of small New York clubs rather than risk submitting himself to another insult.

When Sandy called, badgering me and claiming that this would be, by far, the best new guest we could have on the show, I naturally had some reservations. Still, I called in Rudy Tellez and tried to convince him that it sounded like a good idea. Rudy walked in, picked up some press releases on Tiny, and then said into the phone, "Sandy, tell me what this is again." Sandy repeated the story. Rudy looked at me and said those inimitable words. "Well, it's your neck kid." And I promptly scheduled Tiny.

Just having him walk through the office on his first visit—a white-faced Baby Huey with the shopping bag and the ukelele neck sticking out of it and his mincing little gait—was enough to send everybody in "The Tonight Show" offices into shock, and enough to make *me* feel a little leery, too. He came in and sat down and we started the interview. Everything—but everything—he said made me laugh. I felt embarrassed by this, but he didn't seem the least bit concerned—as a matter of fact, he seemed pleased by my attentiveness. He always referred to me as "Mr. Tennis." I never could get on a first-name basis with Tiny, and in the end, neither could Johnny. The interview increased my anxiety, I admit, but it also increased my obsessive curiosity about what impression this character might be able to make on an unsuspecting audience. To my relief, I was able to turn out seven or eight pages of good notes, and then Tiny had to go down to the studio and rehearse. I went with him. The highly conservative, Archie Bunker-like stage crew instantly disliked him, and when Tiny first began to rehearse "Tiptoe Through the Tulips," they were appalled and shocked. I was nervous, but I knew it would play one of two ways: it would either go down as *the* most disastrous moment in ten years of broadcasting on "The Tonight Show," or it would score as something monumental.

My anxieties continued to mount throughout the

day, and by the time Tiny's segment approached, I was regarded as something of a leper. No one on the staff would stand next to me; they didn't want to be associated with me when this thing went right into the toilet and I was drummed forever from the network. At last, Johnny gave Tiny his introduction, and out he minced, blowing kisses and looking blank. He missed his mark, wandered around, started to twang his ukelele, and then—in that incredible falsetto voice—began singing "Tiptoe." The audience went into absolute shock, but Johnny was ready for them —he did three takes to break them up, and the spot was off and running. Every time Tiny would hit a really high falsetto note, Johnny would do a wild eye-take and the audience would fall apart. Tiny came over and sat down, and as Johnny asked him a series of questions, a star was literally born there on "The Tonight Show."

If it's true that for every action there is an opposite and equal reaction, this was cerainly the night that proved it. While "The Tonight Show" home audience was laughing hysterically at Tiny Tim, those watching the other stations were being depressed by the news specials dealing with the assassination of Martin Luther King. I know Johnny was distraught that he appeared so callous as to have had Tiny Tim on his show while a man he genuinely admired was being eulogized everywhere else on the air. The following night Johnny did not do his monologue for the first time in history, but rather repeated an appearance Martin Luther King had recently made on the show on a night Harry Belafonte had guest-hosted. But, nevertheless, people on the street were talking about it for days afterward, and Johnny, of course, insisted that Tiny be back in ten days to see just how long this could keep going. (Eventually, of course, Tiny had his wedding on the air and the show captured something like an 85 percent share—the most incredible audience "The Tonight Show" had ever attracted. We heard later that all the monitors backstage at "The Merv Griffin

Show," which taped the same time we did, were tuned to the wedding because no one there wanted to miss it.)

My recollections of Tiny are bittersweet. He contributed greatly to my credibility on "The Tonight Show"—but I was upset to see his career wane and to watch him fall back into very nearly the same oblivion from which he had come. He claims to have no regrets and to feel only appreciation for the time he had at the top, but there is a tragedy in the fact that neither he nor his "professional" representatives were wise enough to put some money aside for him. I sometimes think there should be a law, comparable to the Coogan law, in which performers and prize-fighters without the wisdom to protect themselves have money set aside for them in trust.

My last note on Tiny concerns an incident very revealing of his character that shocked everyone on the show. I don't recall the exact song Tiny did, but I know it was a patriotic medley, something like "The Stars and Stripes Forever" with "Onward, Christian Soldiers." Some of the audience laughed at the medley, and when it was over, we watched open-mouthed as Tiny berated them fiercely, shaking his clenched fists over his head. Tiny, it turned out, was a highly conservative, ultra-right-wing patriot, and he meant exactly what he sang.

One of the best things to come out of the Tiny Tim era for me was a certain confidence in Johnny Carson's basic humanity. Although he always managed to get considerable humorous mileage out of Tiny—but not at Tiny's expense—he never contemplated humiliating Tiny even if it would have benefited his position comedically. In fact, Johnny was always extremely polite to Tiny, and I liked him a lot for that.

The Pre-Interview

The audience for this show is East Jesus, Illinois. Don't say East Jesus, say Joliet.

—RUDY TELLEZ

In addition to finding and developing new long-term talent, the coordinator had another major responsibility: to screen the guests before the show and develop for Johnny those few interview questions that would preserve his image as a warm, inventive, and interested host. After all, one cannot expect any host, let alone Johnny, to come out four or five nights a week, ask hundreds of questions, and have all of them generate even moderately fresh or unusual answers. But fresh and unusual answers are what make people watch talk shows. Consequently, it is the job of the talent coordinator to find the meat in the guests' stories and to bypass as much as possible the time-consuming deadwood that the host would otherwise have to chop through. Johnny doesn't use the prepared question in any sense as a script, and will commonly deviate from the written questions. That is a habit, by the way, that can be discouraging for both the coordinators and the guests. If Johnny goes off the track into an area which has not been first cleared of "fat," the guest's answer is apt to come back either boring or nonsensical. When that happens, Johnny can invariably be heard complaining, in the rap meeting, "Boy, was that person dull; I don't ever want that person back on the show."

Most of the time, pre-interviews were routine. Once you'd established that a guest was desirable—that is, "entertaining" and possessed of "rapport"—it was just a matter of how much time you had to spend with him or her to nail down five or six interesting tangents to fill the segment. There were a few things that would break the monotony of this routine for me.

Occasionally, I would agree to do a pre-interview at a performer's home, an arrangement that was obviously more time-consuming, but that was also invariably more interesting, since it gave me a chance to study the person in his natural environment—almost like a form of wildlife, which in many cases was close to the truth. A good example was David Carradine. At the height of his television series, "Kung Fu," it was arranged that David would make his first appearance on "The Tonight Show," and I, counting myself lucky to have drawn him as a guest, made arrangements to visit him at his house in Laurel Canyon (in the Hollywood hills). At the time, he was cohabitating with a beautiful young actress by the name of Barbara Hershey Seagull whom I had met years before in New York. The couple and their son, Free, along with four or five friendly flea-infested dogs, lived in what looked for all the world like a squatter's cabin in the trees. It was not the kind of house in which you'd expect to find the star of one of the top two or three shows on television. It had little rooms tacked on haphazardly here and there, and, while Barbara seemed to make at least a cursory effort at housekeeping, David managed to continually undo it all. To call theirs a casual life-style would be understating the case—David wore nothing but a pair of soiled Levi's, Barbara wore a plain Indian cotton shift, and Free wore nothing at all except his own feces down the insides of his legs. David has a reputation for being more than slightly iconoclastic. He had a strange childhood, without question. His father, John, is himself great material for the analyst's couch, and the stories about the family as a whole challenge the Barrymore legends. But David seems to genuinely like people, and as we chatted and found things in common, it became harder and harder to get away. By the time I fled off through the trees with a ream of notes, I was hopelessly late. I put a lot of effort into David's interview questions, but Johnny took an immediate dislike to his unorthodox looks, and the segment came out noticeably hostile. I remember feeling bewildered about that, because Johnny doesn't usually allow personal preferences to get in the way of entertainment—especially once it's gotten on camera. Even after that, I still thought David would make a good potential interview, and I hit on the idea of trying him again when George Carlin, with whom I felt he'd have a lot in common, next guest-hosted the show. Another bomb. David and George never once were able to say anything that the other could understand. I was forced to give up on Carradine for the time being.

Of all the guests I worked with, I think the one I was most surprised to find that I really genuinely liked was Raquel Welch. My first pre-interview with her was at her hotel, and after that I would *always* go out of my way to meet her at her convenience, on her own turf—she deserved it. The first time I visited her, she was ensconced in a huge suite at the Plaza Hotel in New York. She came to the door herself, dressed in simple slacks, a sexy blouse, and a boy's cap with her hair tucked into it. She had no makeup on, and even with a scrubbed face she was an absolute traffic-stopper. It was the first time I'd seen her minus all the theatrical flash, and I found her to be even more radiant than she was in her sex-symbol role—especially in the eyes, which are like tilted chameleon's eyes. She kindly ignored my thunderstruck look and led me into the sitting area, where her press agent and manager awaited. We got down to work. I remember being immediately surprised at her candor and openness, and was later exhilarated when she made an excellent appearance on the show.

The next time I met her was years later, on another interview—this time at the Waldorf Towers. Again I can remember in detail how she looked—a tailored white pantsuit, light makeup, and flowing hair. Again she talked candidly and openly, and I was impressed by the obvious effort she had made in the years since I last saw her to educate herself, to become a better conversationalist and a more well-rounded person. She had succeeded on all counts, and we got so engrossed in our private discussion that I ended up with enough good notes for four or five appearances instead of just one. From the time I realized I was late and got up to leave to the time I actually got into the elevator, 45 minutes must have passed; we couldn't stop talking. To this day I regret not having thought better of rushing back, but I'll certainly never know what might have happened. We had a very comfortable association, and as the hair on my chest turns gray at an alarming rate, I like to fantasize that it might have developed into something more. Raquel was one of those ladies whom I always thought was unfairly branded for life as having large bustlines and small I.Q.'s. On the other hand, some beauties like Jill St. John have garnered reputations as intellectuals, but if you pin them down, you find that, in fact, they have very little to say that justifies that image.

The single greatest disappointment I had during my tenure on the show was the fact that no luscious blonde ever came up to me, looked me straight in the eye, and said, "I will do anything to be on 'The Tonight Show.'" Not that I know what I'd have done, but it would have been flattering to hear the offer, anyway. I must admit that I never used "The Tonight Show" for a "score," even though situations occasionally arose that could have been pushed in that direction.

Besides sexual temptations, there are other, more

tangible offerings that present themselves to coordinators—some of them legal and some of them not. First of all, there are the "freebies." For freebies, working "The Tonight Show" in New York had great advantages over working in L.A. For one thing, there are many more clubs and theaters and shows to see there, all of which, if you play it carefully in terms of ethics, you never have to pay to see. Press agents representing Broadway shows are dying to have one or two of their stars on "The Tonight Show," and as an inducement—and an appetite-whetter—they will say, "What night would you like to come to the theater? I'll have two tickets waiting." So there you are with your date, sitting fourth-row center on "press comps." If the show was in a nightclub, the whole check would be picked up, which made the arrangement a great way to impress girls. In Los Angeles, on the other hand, people are cheap (ask anyone who lives on tips); it's rare to have a free ticket or to have the tab picked up, and what's more, all the theaters and clubs are inconvenient to get to (*everything* is out of the way in L.A.).

Now, "freebies" are a special category of fringe benefits; to qualify as a legal freebie, the offering has to be both directly work-related and inexpensive. That really limits the field to nightclubs and shows, books, records, and screening passes. The no-man's-land that lies just beyond freebies is known as payola. Payola is something that is directly work-related but that is *not* inexpensive—in other words, it includes inducement above and beyond the call of what's really needed to do your job. In California, there was never any temptation to slide into what could be construed as a payola situation, because if they were too tight to offer a theater ticket, you can be sure they weren't going to blow "real" money on a junket.

Not so in New York. I can well remember in the early days back there having to shy away from people with attractive offers. It was not uncommon for an agent to casually say, "Hey, I've got a great act working in Jamaica. Why don't you fly down for the weekend as my guest and see the show?" That sort of thing was, of course, verboten, although an occasional trip to Las Vegas for the same thing might get the go-ahead from the producer.

Beyond the land of payola and freebies lies out-and-out bribery, and *those* offers weren't uncommon on *either* coast. As I recall, *my* first initiation into the world of bribes came in the form of a short lecture from Rudy. He told me, "You will be offered money and other considerations now and then in exchange for booking acts. If you take it and get caught, you will not only be out of a job, you will probably be out of the business permanently." He went on to suggest, and I thought this wise counsel, that if I were thinking of selling out, I should set my goal high—he suggested $250,000 as a round figure.

Seven years later, I got a call from a man who wanted a favor. He laid his plan right on the line. He said, "What would it cost me to get this singer on 'The Tonight Show'?"

I replied, flippantly, "Well, *my* figure is a quarter of a million dollars."

He hesitated for a moment and then, in a quiet voice, he said, "Do you want it in cash or a certified check?"

Since we coordinators were not allowed the harmless fun of lining our pockets with baksheesh from would-be stars, we were forced to relieve the tedium of our jobs in more creative ways. One of the things that produced the most hilarious results was sifting through the mountains of pitch letters, phone calls, and articles sent to us daily by America's cranks and finding those few off-the-wall oddball spots that would continue to set "The Tonight Show" apart from the rest of the talk shows. How we found these little gems was really up to our own imaginations. (Since many of these oddball spots did not turn out to be cute once on the air, I prefer to remind you only of those that were smashing successes.)

One of the best of these came from a simple newspaper clipping—a human-interest "filler" that positively fascinated me. I tracked down the fellow in the clipping and made the booking, asking no one's permission. I then tacked a card up on the booking board which said only one word: "DOMINOES." Everybody was then certain I had lost my mind. They hung around like vultures, waiting for the show to come so they could see me go into the "porcelain facility" with this weird stunt, whatever it might be. The day of the taping, a fellow came in well before the normal time and spent six hours setting up dominoes in an exotic pattern on the floor. After doing a brief interview with the high school student, Johnny gently tipped over the first domino and then down they all went—7,500 dominoes, one after the other—with an effect like wind rippling through wheat fields. It was exquisite. It was also so successful that the footage is now frequently used on anniversary specials.

The "oddball booking" that I liked the most came as a result of a tape cassette sent to me from a local show in Madison, Wisconsin. Usually, those tapes are of the station manager's tap-dancing niece, and you look them over, wrap them back up, and return them with a polite note of refusal. This tape, though, absolutely destroyed me, and I immediately made arrangements to get what was in it onto "The Tonight Show." The man who came out from Madison, Wisconsin, was a very clean-cut, wholesome-looking guy, and a practicing attorney in a good firm back there. But he had this hobby: manualism—that is, by pressing his palms together, he could create implosions and explosions of air, and through practice he was able to somehow turn these farting noises into a recognizable melody. As I had calculated, it was the exact kind of thing that blew Johnny's mind, and the man was asked back several times.

In the pursuit of these bookings, there would often be close calls, since some of the things that sounded like "fun-oddball" were just *plain* oddball, instead.

There was one pathetic act floating around the periphery of television for a while that may even have gotten booked elsewhere, and this came to us on a recommendation. It consisted of a man and his "trained" pig. At least the man *claimed* the pig was trained. As it happened, the pig wasn't so much trained as tortured. The man insisted that the pig could actually sing, and to prove it, he grabbed the pig under his arm, announced the "Blue Danube Waltz," and struck up the music. As the pig oink-oinked rhythmically along, it became apparent that he wasn't oinking to the music; he was squealing in time to having his testicles squeezed by the "trainer." Somehow, someone realized that this must have been excruciating for the pig, and we did manage to avoid booking the act.

The worst day I ever had on "The Tonight Show" occurred in New York. There were four guests on that night, and I was responsible for two of them. Neither had ever done the show before. Problems started in the afternoon with a musical-comedy act, The New Zealand Trading Company, made up of Australian aborigines and kiwis. I'd been assured that a federal work permit had been obtained for the show since they were foreigners. They came in and set up, rehearsed, and were wonderfully cooperative for a musical group. The word then came down from our legal department that not only had they apparently not gotten a work permit, but their visas had expired, so the U.S. Immigration Department had given them 12 hours to leave the country. They fled the studio for the Commonwealth country of Canada, and we were now short an act—first crisis. Second crisis— Johnny finished his monologue, the only totally sacred portion of the show, never to be disturbed or interrupted in any way. As he was announcing his guests, just before the first commercial, he said the name of my other responsibility, Louisa Moritz. Louisa is a well-endowed, blue-eyed, blond Cuban, with a tiny voice and gigantic ambition. When she heard Johnny say her name, she thought she was being introduced and so she walked right out onstage. Johnny looked horrified, until she told him who she was, and then he broke up, fortunately. However, my stomach lining is still on the mend.

On another occasion, I got a call from the man who was doing public relations for *Hustler* magazine, that infamous publication out of Indiana. He had a proposition for us. Now, this man had called many times before, and each of his proposals had been, let's say, extremely easy to turn down. However, this one gave me pause. If you'll recall, *Hustler* really made its name when it ran those full-page color nude shots of Jacqueline Kennedy Onassis that had been taken surreptitiously on a Greek island. The pictures were fuzzy and practically amateur, but they definitely had shock value and sold a lot of magazines. Jacqueline Onassis must have been enraged, but much to Larry Flynt's dismay, she never sued the magazine. If she had, *Hustler* would have netted even more publicity and sales revenue than they did. As sort of a desperation move, Flynt's people called us up and said, "How would you like to have Jackie Kennedy on 'The Tonight Show'?"

To which I replied, "Is it April the first *already?* I mean, how do you expect to persuade her to do *anything* for you after that stunt with the pictures—not that she would have before, mind you?"

He said, "Well, I'm going to send you a Xeroxed copy of a cashier's check for one million dollars written in her name, which we will give to her or her favorite charity if she will come on the show and answer just *one* question about the article and pictures that appeared in *Hustler.*"

I thought about that one for a minute and then said, "Well, I won't tell you no, but the mechanics of it are entirely up to you—I'm not touching it." I didn't exactly wait by the phone to hear the outcome—and I was not surprised when no call came. *Hustler,* I am sure, never got a chance to leave its full name on the answering service.

No doubt the worst talent-scouting experience I ever had was during one of the notorious California trips. The staff sometimes stayed at the Continental Hyatt House on Sunset Strip, and when outsiders learned that, they would naturally assume that Johnny stayed there, too. Now, there's no way Johnny would have stayed in a hotel like that; it used to cater to performers and destructive rock acts and was known around town as the Continental Riot House. He always went to the Bel Air Hotel, or some quiet spot—but messages kept coming in for him, nevertheless. Most of them would go to crazy John Carsey (because of the name resemblance) and he would sort through them and keep the bizarre ones for his scrapbook. We used to go over them, fortified with a couple of drinks, and have a roaring good time at these poor people's expense.

On my first trip West, after a mere three weeks on the show, John brought a message over to me and, appearing to be totally earnest, said, "Now, here's one I think you should definitely follow up on."

It was from a woman who lived alone and who felt she should definitely be on the show and blah-blah-blah. Well, being new at the game and a fool to boot, I took Carsey at his word and called her for an appointment. I must admit that she sounded crazy enough to be a potential guest, but she said she couldn't come out to the Hyatt House for an interview, so I had to agree to come to her apartment in Hollywood.

I remember thinking, "Oh-oh—here's trouble." But I said okay, nevertheless. So, one evening after a taping, I drove out to the area. I had a hard time finding the place, because I was automatically looking for a decent building. In actuality, my destination turned out to be a tacky residence hotel in which the lobby decor consisted of a rickety desk and an even more rickety old man. I asked him where the house phones were and he just snorted.

I gave him the name of the woman I was supposed to see and he said, "Oh, *sure*—go right on up," with a sneer that indicated he knew something *I* didn't.

What answered my knock was a woman of about 40—but going on 80—who had tried to put on makeup but who had failed abysmally and had wound up with lipstick running from ear to ear. With her lipstick or without it, we had a pathetic case here.

I instantly had the urge to run, but she said, "Sit down, sit down—let me get you a drink."

I decided to decline her generosity, since the only drink in sight was the bourbon she was swilling straight from the bottle, and quickly I got around to saying, "Well, tell me—why is it you want to be on the show?"

She replied, "I'm absolutely fascinating. I have wonderful stories to tell." And with that, she rattled off a series of tales that would have made even a "soap opera" editor shudder. Finally, she said, "I am also a terrific singer."

And I said, relieved, "Well, do you have any tapes? Will you be working anyplace where I can come by and hear you?" She said, "Oh, no—I'm going to audition for you *now*."

And I said, "Oh . . . okay," thinking that as soon as she finished eight bars, I could get the hell out of there, have a drink, go find Carsey—and tear him limb from limb. But the woman kept stalling. Finally, I had to say, "Well, aren't you going to sing for me? I really do have another appointment [meaning Carsey]."

She said, "Well, okay," and then disappeared into the bathroom—where she began to sing. Finally, I understood. The woman had discovered one of those secrets everybody knows: that the acoustics in a tiled bathroom are sensational and make even the worst singer in the world sound adequate. As it happened, there wasn't enough tile in all of Italy to make *this* woman sound adequate, and Carsey has since learned to live with his plastic kneecaps.

The grief of being put in a rotten position like that didn't end even after I left the show. I had been gone for a good 18 months when another impromptu audition occurred without my consent. I was in the housewares section of Bullocks department store one day, minding my own business and making a few humble purchases. I gave the girl at the counter my charge card, and as she ran it through she glanced at the name and said, "Oh! It's very nice to meet you—how do I audition for 'The Tonight Show'?" I was stunned. I couldn't imagine how anyone who didn't know me personally could possibly be familiar with my name, but before I could recover and escape through a side door into the toy department, three other saleswomen were at the girl's elbow, cornering and badgering me about what a great singer this girl was, and how I should really put her on the show. I tried to explain that I was no longer *with* the show, but to no avail. I ended up backing out the door with my pots and pans, mumbling incoherently and staring while the girl wailed out "Feelings" right there in the middle of the housewares section.

Egos on Parade

It's Plugsville.

—Tony Randall

In spite of the fact that "The Tonight Show" is in a way just another "jaw fest"—a frothy piece of entertainment—and in spite of the fact that everyone who does it, no matter how big or small, gets the same, low S.A.G. scale fee (to the eternal disgust of semi-regulars like Jonathan Winters), a guest spot on "The Tonight Show" does carry with it a certain undeniable prestige.

For ambitious people in any field, it represents their "arrival" on the national scene; for aspiring performers, the show is usually the biggest and most crucial booking in their young careers; and for already established stars, it's a chance to promote whatever they want to 15,000,000 people—for free.

Curiously it's the very impact of that audience figure that causes many entertainers with solid careers to balk at doing the show at all. They know there's a real danger that when the audience sees them face to face, it will be disillusionment time. A star who has great power at the box office, for example, usually helps hold onto it by maintaining a certain mystique with the public; when the people who pay $4 a head to see them in the movies find out that they drink beer, watch TV, and fight with their spouses just like everyone else, it sort of takes the edge off.

As much as the talent coordinators can appreciate the wisdom of a star who chooses to keep a low profile, every one of them still wishes he could find the magic word that would convince a McQueen or a Redford or a Cary Grant to just once break his silence. It almost never happened. I think their sentiments were summed up best by a conversation I once had with Gilbert Roland.

Gilbert Roland had always been one of my favorite actors, and one day, on a hunch, I decided to call and find out why he had never done the show. My coordinator's instincts told me that Mr. Roland's on-screen personality and qualities were probably a carry-over from his personal life, and I thought that booking him would be a real coup. When I called, he answered his own phone—something unheard of in show business —and we chatted briefly. But then, to my surprise, when I asked him to come on the show, he said that he was extremely charmed and flattered by my offer and was thankful for my kind words, but—he had been getting away with his "act" in film and television for the past 40 years, and he had absolutely no desire to go on "The Tonight Show," risk bombing, and blow a career that had successfully taken in a lot of people for a great many years. How can you argue with the logic of a man like that? You shouldn't, and I didn't.

You never know, though, when some of the big names who you thought would never do the show will suddenly, for personal reasons, agree to appear. They don't do it on a whim; they have their own motives. Usually they want to plug either a charity they're about to do a benefit for, or a film, starring them, that they've sunk their own capital into or have a percentage of. Still, as I say, you never know. In one instance that I remember, a call came to me from the press representative of the Franklin Mint in Philadelphia. He explained that the Mint was putting out a series of prints of paintings by 15 or so different performers—people like Red Skelton, Henry Fonda, and Elke Sommer, who are not immediately identified as painters—and he said the Mint would like to have the paintings displayed on "The Tonight Show."

I said, "Well, that's an awful lot of commercial content on behalf of the Franklin Mint, you know. . . ."

And he said, "No, no—the series is already sold out. We just think they're terribly good and that people would like to see them."

I said, "Well, who were you suggesting as a spokesperson?"

He replied, "Henry Fonda."

I just laughed. Then I said, cockily, "Listen, if you can deliver Henry Fonda I can *guarantee* you we'll do the spot."

The irony turned out to be that Fonda, who avoids talk shows like the plague, actually wants to be thought of as a painter (and he is a brilliant and gifted painter), so he was eager to come on and do the show in the artist's role.

On the flip side, there are a few shows in my recollection in which the problem wasn't a lack of big stars, but actually an over-abundance of them. Oddly, one of the most potentially dangerous situations to have on a talk show is a lineup of guests in which each name is as big as the last—particularly if they're all in the same line, like comedy. It takes a real will to win to be successful in this business, and winners, when they're lined up together, are like a bunch of thoroughbreds; the competition can be fierce. If everything goes the right way, on the other hand, those shows can be absolute blockbusters. One of the most famous shows in that category involved Bob Hope, Dean Martin, and George Gobel, every one of whom is also an experienced scene-stealer. Hope came on first and was excellent. Martin came out next and did his ingratiating drunk routine, pretending not to know who Johnny was and asking repeatedly when Carson was going to appear. When it was George Gobel's turn, he knew he had a tough row to hoe to get any action away from Hope and Martin, but he came through—in fact, he managed to produce a line which has since become one of the all-time "Tonight Show" classics. In the middle of a story, he turned to Johnny and said, "Do you ever feel that the entire world is a tuxedo and you're a pair of brown shoes?" Of course, that got an uproarious laugh, and Gobel was in heaven, thinking he had finally carved out a spot. He didn't, however, really have the last laugh; unbeknownst to George, during his entire routine, and in full view of the audience, Dean had been steadily flicking his cigarette ashes into George's Scotch. Showmanship, let's face it, will out.

Friendly practical joking and one-upsmanship among peers is one of show business's most popular sports. One practical joke I remember well concerned an accident Johnny had on his slant board several years ago and which put him in a whiplash collar. He had been working out on the board when it had suddenly collapsed, dumping him onto the back of his neck and causing him no small amount of agony and nerve damage. He had even been forced to miss the show for a while, his mobility was so seriously impaired. (He blamed the accident on faulty equipment and had sued both the manufacturer and the retailer for a sum which would be outrageous by anyone else's standards.) Anyway, he had to wear a whiplash collar.

At the same time Johnny was imprisoned in *his* collar, Harvey Korman happened to be wearing one, too—his being the result of a body-surfing accident at Malibu. Johnny heard about Harvey's collar and decided it would be good fun to ask Harvey to come on the show to compare injuries. Harvey, who's always a very reluctant talk-show guest, agreed to come on; the idea of the two of them sitting around bitching about their mutual pains, like two old maids yakking about their gallstone operations—appealed to him and he also knew a guaranteed laugh when he saw one.

Harvey's two best friends at the time were McLean Stevenson and Tim Conway, and when they heard from Harvey that Johnny had invited him to dinner after the taping at one of Johnny's favorite restaurants, Dan Tana's, they went into action. McLean and Tim are constitutionally incapable of allowing the world to take its own straight course, and so they decided to join Harvey and Johnny for dinner—but not in any normal, adult way. They went out and rented white doctors' uniforms, complete with the bags and the stethoscopes, and then went and sat in Dan Tana's waiting for their prey, Johnny and Harvey, to show up in the whiplash collars. They went to a table and parked, explaining to the maître d' that it was okay, they were expecting Johnny Carson and Harvey Korman. Well, they waited. Then they waited some more. Half an hour passed, and the maître d' began to get a little snippy about their squatting at one of his best tables, but they protested: "No, really—Johnny Carson is coming in for dinner." Eventually, after something like an hour had passed, it began to dawn on Tim and McLean that perhaps the practical joke was in fact on them, and they managed to skulk out, looking and feeling, in their little ambulance outfits, like the lunatics they are.

The Green Room

I see you've rearranged your dirt.

—JOHNNY CARSON

Sitting backstage at the show is a wonderful vantage point from which to pick up on little show-business customs and hypocrisies.

There is, for example, an almost ironclad division between the world of a motion-picture performer and the world of a television performer; in fact, for all they see of each other, they might as well be a fence painter and a grocer. I remember one time when I had booked Don Adams (at the peak of his popularity with "Get Smart") on a show on which Kirk Douglas was also a guest. Kirk came over and pulled me aside before the taping and said, "Craig, would it be possible for you to introduce me to Don Adams?"

I thought at first that he was kidding and just chuckled conspiratorially. When I realized he was earnest, I said, "What? Don't you know Don?"

Kirk looked puzzled and said, as though it should have been obvious to me, "Why, no—he's in television and I'm in movies."

In the realm of hypocrisy, there have been some

beauties. A fellow once came on the show with a routine which must have been part of a promotional for the lobster industry—I don't remember. Anyway, his "partner" in the routine was a gigantic, 25-pound lobster, which he continually petted and talked to, treating it like a favorite German shepherd.

After the show, the man was on his way out the door when someone yelled out in panic, "Hey, Mister, you forgot your friend!"

Without even missing a step, the man shot over his shoulder, "Oh, yeah—anyone who wants it, take it!"

Well, Jeannie Pryor and Mike Zannella decided to spirit the lobster back to Jeannie's small apartment and make dinner of it. Of course the lobster was so huge it wouldn't even go in a pot, and Jeannie and Mike had to chase it around the living room, hitting it over the head with a hammer, trying to get it to die so they could cook it. Eventually, they managed to prepare it, and they sat down to dinner in front of—what else? —"The Tonight Show." What happened, of course, is that they found themselves dismantling and consuming one of the show's star guests as they calmly watched his pre-taped performance on the small screen. (It's been suggested that two-legged guests have found themselves in similar situations since, but no one will be too specific.)

I remember once when the famed nutritionist and health expert, Adele Davis, was on the show proclaiming herself a vegetarian and discussing at great length the importance of eating only the proper foods. Her appearance happened to coincide with a night when an anniversary celebration of some kind was going on backstage, so when the show was finished taping, the caterers rolled out steam trays loaded with delicious "junk" food—deep-fried shrimp, barbequed chicken wings, cocktail sausages, and other assorted non-digestibles—which lesser-educated palates than Ms. Davis's tend to relish. To my shock, Ms. Davis rushed the carts (she was the first person in line) and wolfed down more fat-saturated meat than any other three people in the studio combined!

But the best incident, in terms of sheer shock value for me, concerned two New York policemen. They were a highly successful vice team that had affected the monikers "Batman" and "Robin," in honor of their style of arrest, which the Brooklyn street people described as "swooping down out of nowhere." They also had singularly undistinguished records at the police academy, since they believed that almost everything they were being fed from the book was of little or no value when it came to making busts out on the street. They were notorious for bending police rules to get the job done, and so they naturally had a much more impressive record than your average book-toting "guardian of safety." As it happened, they liked to bend the law in some ways that weren't exactly job-connected. I remember popping into their dressing room to say hello prior to their appearance on the show and finding myself blinded by a blue haze of marijuana smoke. I managed to fight my way into the room and there I saw the two of them sitting on the couch passing a huge, outsized grass pipe back and forth in order, they told me, to make sure they would be nicely "relaxed" for the show.

Getting "loose" before the show, whether it's on grass or booze or whatever, is not such an uncommon thing for performers to do. It's a tense situation out there, and getting loaded is at least one sure way of reducing unbearable nerve activity, but, unfortunately, also reducing their timing, judgment, and sensibilities. When the show first visited California, the "powers" decided that it might be a nice gesture to have an open bar for performers in the "green room" backstage. Now, the green room, a theatrical tradition dating back to before the Elizabethan theater, is an area offstage where each performer and his entourage can sit with all the other performers and *their* entourages and get rowdy and relaxed before they go on. At the same time, they can watch the show progress on the monitor and pick up the feel of the way it's going before their segments. (The green room, by the way, is almost never green—in the case of "The Tonight Show," it's sort of a dirty beige, but never mind.) On the second night the bar was in effect, the star guest —making a very rare appearance, indeed—was Marlon Brando. When Johnny introduced Marlon, with great fanfare, the curtains opened and out came one of the greatest actors in history, stumbling across the stage as blind on champagne as you can get and still be able to stumble. Marlon already mumbles a lot when he's in a T-shirt and sober on screen, but that's like Lord Olivier compared to Marlon sloshed on champagne and trying to carry on a regular conversation. It was not a rewarding interview. By no coincidence, the open bar in the green room was gone by the next night, never to return. But there is always a discreet bar concealed in a prop box offstage, and of course there are the dressing rooms, so performers, being as they are very creative, have never exactly had to do without, if booze was their thing.

The dressing rooms are a story in themselves. True to NBC's economic form—and in spite of the fact that they've got the most important performers in show business appearing for $458.75 a throw—the dressing rooms that line the hallways of "The Tonight Show" studio are tacky, tiny cubicles, sparsely furnished, rarely clean, and far from conducive to any sort of theatrical preparation. Why the guests have not mutinied by now is beyond me. The theoretically better dressing rooms—the ones on the same floor as the stage, and especially those near the makeup room —are reserved for the performers with the most status, and for the guest host, if there is one. Those guests who don't qualify are relegated to little dungeon rooms or attic hovels that, really, you'd better have all your shots to walk into. Some of the older performers, over the hill as far as their star status is concerned, can usually be heard bitching loudly about having to climb the stairs, and they wonder, irately, why they weren't put in a first-floor dressing room commensurate with their stature. Billy de Wolfe used to have a whole "Tonight Show" routine based on the fact that he had a basement dressing room, and every time someone flushed the toilet, the walls reverberated so badly that he feared for his life.

Anyway, there were often guests who did in fact want to drink, but they rarely liked to do it all alone in their dressing rooms. One of the best of this group was Elaine Stritch, the legendary Broadway actress. Elaine has a sense of humor that's biting and hip; she was once a drinker of some repute, so you can guess what that added up to. She used to come to the studio early and make the rounds with her nasty little dachshund, a creature that would invariably bark at and bite anybody who came within its range. Then she'd park the dog in the dressing room and start on a pint bottle of brandy, ultimately spending the whole afternoon wandering the halls of NBC, wearing nothing but a man's shirt, spiked heels, and carrying a half-empty bottle. (Actually, Elaine has great legs, so nobody ever objected.) On one of Elaine's appearances, Lee Trevino was also a guest, and before air time, she and Lee sat for a long time in the green room, joking and sharing Elaine's brandy. Elaine went on before Lee, and after 10 or 12 minutes out there—in which she was even more bizarre than usual—I could see in Johnny's face that he was thinking, "Oh boy, I'd better get Elaine out of here and go to a nice, sedate golfer. Lee is calm; he'll settle the show back down."

So we went to a commercial, and as soon as it was over, Johnny introduced Lee. As he did, Lee came wandering out onstage, practically broadcasting the fact that he, too, had been drinking. His hair was a mess, his tie askew, and one shirttail was trailing out of his pants. The first thing he did was to take a wrong turn, and he staggered halfway to the band before realizing the problem and changing course. The look on Johnny's face was simply incredulous—he'd never seen Lee in any way but dapper and together. Here he'd gotten rid of Elaine to get some sanity, and Lee was, if anything, worse off than she. When Lee finally sat down, he was charming and funny and giggling a lot—but Elaine kept interrupting, announcing that she and "José" had gotten engaged in the green room while waiting to go on. Johnny just sat there squirming slightly and doing lots of eye-takes at the camera while Lee struggled with Elaine, trying to get back the ring he had given her in a moment of abandon, while Elaine bellowed, "No chance, José—I haven't been engaged in 24 years!"

Among the moments of plain, flat-out panic I remember on "The Tonight Show," one definitely stands out as the most unpredictable. The guest and perpetrator was Alan Garfield, a really superb actor and a good New York radical Jew with a lunatic sense of humor. When I first met Alan, he had just gotten married to a red-haired Irish Catholic girl he'd met in a fight over a phone booth. The marriage, of course, was destined to go the way of a great Stiller and Meara routine, but Alan was thrilled with it then. He was introduced as a distinguished actor, came out, and proceeded to talk very sanely with Johnny. Johnny congratulated him on his new marriage, and Alan smiled and said, "Yeah, I've got to show you how terrific my wife is, Johnny." And with that he stood up, opened his shirt, unbuckled his belt, dropped his pants to his ankles and, revealing grossly heavy thighs, pointed proudly to the matching blue bikini and tanktop underwear set she had bought for him. Well, Johnny froze solid. For a long moment there was no other sound in the studio but the strains of Alan's wife slowly screaming from somewhere out in the darkened audience.

Sometimes the guests did things that weren't so cute —in fact, they were downright hostile. One extraordinarily talented actress who can be brutal and funny at the same time is Lee Grant. During the short-lived run of her NBC series, "Faye," Lee—who is certainly a good guest for the show and can be mesmerizing even when playing herself, wanted to go on to talk about the series. Of course we booked her, but on the day she was to appear, word came down to us that NBC had canceled her series. Now none of us could determine if Lee knew, and it was a sure thing that we weren't going to mention it in the interview, but for the entire time she was on the air, Johnny's mouth kept curling ever so slightly at the fact that Lee was knocking herself out for a show that had actually ceased to exist. Toward the end of her segment, she showed an exceptionally charming film clip from the show—something that would really make you want to watch it—and then said, in a very polite and ladylike way, "Well, I hope you liked that, but I think I should tell you at this point that an hour before we came into the studio, I got a call letting me know that the series has been canceled. You'd think they would have had the sense to wait until after I made this appearance to tell me that, but they are a cold, thoughtless group of people."

Johnny, when he had recovered himself, said, "Who canceled it?"

And Lee replied, "Well, there's a man named Marvin Antonowski—known as the 'Mad Programmer'—and he scratched the show." Lee remained very charming about the whole issue, but in her understatement the bitterness was obvious. At the end of the interview, she announced, "Nevertheless, I would like all of you to go on watching the show, because it's good. In fact, get all your friends to watch the show, because that way maybe in the last few weeks we'll have spectacular ratings. If that happens, you see, then the Mad Programmer will have to call me and say, 'Listen, Lee, your show has become a big hit. Won't you stay on and finish the series?' At which point I can give him this. . . ." And with that, right there on camera, she flipped Mr. Antonowski, in absentia, the proverbial "bird." Well, the audience shrieked their pleasure en masse, the censors tried to drown themselves in the drinking fountains, and we all howled with joy.

By the way, from the night that show aired, Marvin Antonowski was forever branded in the business as the "Mad Programmer," and that onus was what, I am sure, contributed to the abrupt termination of his NBC career. No doubt his own lack of judgment had made it inevitable, but when the higher-ups in New York heard about the incident (and the indelible handle he had earned for himself), it was for them the crowning blow, and by the end of the broadcast year, Antonowski had been replaced. Another interesting postscript to this episode came when Antonowski called the show the next day to complain about Lee Grant's little character assassination and to demand equal time. When Fred dutifully relayed the message to Johnny, Johnny looked at Fred and, hesitating only briefly, replied, "Tell Mr. Antonowski to go fuck himself."

Bah—Humbug!

Johnny has made a horror of being rude.

—RUDY TELLEZ

One of the most maddening things about show business is the fact that the same ingredient—ego—that makes some talented people into stars makes many others into raving asses. Of course, "The Tonight Show," just by dint of volume, sees more than its share of both types. I remember that one Christmas Johnny and Fred actually decided to hold a contest to see who would receive the most tasteless Christmas card from a celebrity. It was pretty stiff competition that particular year. The card that initially took the lead was from Redd Foxx. The card, which came to Fred, looked like a legitimate Christmas card until you opened it up. Inside there was a picture of Mr. Foxx looking at the rear end of a donkey and underneath was a caption that read: "I hope you have a half-assed Christmas." If that wasn't bad enough for most people's sense of decorum at Christmastime, the photograph also happened to be from the cover of a new record album he was promoting. Actually, it's not the least bit unusual to receive Christmas cards promoting engagements in

Las Vegas and new record albums and books and so forth—press agents have been known to send out Christmas cards announcing the signing of a new client, that sort of thing. Hooray for Hollywood! Anyway, Redd Foxx actually ended up a distant third to the other two major contenders.

Second place went to Rudy Vallee. Rudy immediately won points over Redd because Rudy's Christmas greeting was a postcard. It didn't even get put in an envelope, because you know postcards can be sent much more cheaply than envelopes, a fact which simply reinforced the historical rumor that Rudy Vallee is one of the tightest men who ever walked. Now, to the photograph on the postcard Rudy sent: it showed Rudy and his wife, Ellie, sitting in bed—one of those huge padded numbers that they seem to sell at discount stores—wearing nightclothes and huge grins on their faces to indicate that they were enjoying immensely what they were doing. What they were doing was "reading" a copy of Rudy's new autobiography. So it was not really a Christmas card at all—it was a sales pitch for Rudy's expensive book.

One would normally think that people in a so-called creative business would have, out of necessity, more sensitivity and more taste, but the truth is, most people in the business are sensitive only to their own ego needs. Now, the card that was the flat-out winner—and there wasn't even a discourse on this—was the card sent by Bobby Vinton. This card, I think, would offend anyone, regardless of religious belief—atheist included. Again, it was one of those cheapie postcards —no envelope. On the glossy side was a photograph that appeared to have been taken in Las Vegas (not exactly the Holy Land). It showed Bobby up onstage in an absolutely transfixed state, surrounded below and on all sides by his rapt and adoring fans. Bobby was all dressed in white—very symbolic—but the kicker was the lighting. There was only one spotlight, and it was shining down on him. The spotlight had, if you can bear it, five points, and the effect was that the glow from the "star" enveloped him—you know, much as the star of Bethlehem must have . . . well, you get the idea: the Las Vegas Star of Bethlehem shining on Bobby Vinton from his Christmas postcard.

The kind of maniacal egotism that's funny on Christmas cards is not so funny when it comes into your studio; delusions of grandeur can be a problem.

Once, when actor John Amos was still playing the father on "Good Times"—before his success in "Roots"—we were approached about having him on "The Tonight Show." We agreed, thinking he seemed like a thoughtful, gentle guy. The guest-host on the night he appeared was McLean Stevenson, who had been a friend of John's for years. McLean, in a manner befitting old friends, kidded John about various things, at one point calling him a dumb gorilla or something in an equally Ricklish, harmless vein.

Well, the next day, out of the blue, Fred de Cordova received a wire from John expressing his "great dismay" that a black man would be treated with such low regard on an upstanding program like "The Tonight Show," and basically demanding an apology for his imagined injuries. After the shock wore off, we discovered that, if we had checked around at all, we would have learned that John was regularly aggravated about something—which gives you an idea of how deceptive on-camera appearances can be.

The angriest I have ever seen Johnny Carson become was over an incident involving one of these mammoth "star" ego displays. Although Johnny hates confrontation and will usually avoid "scenes" at all costs, he does have an incredibly quick temper, and I've seen him a few times in a mood of such violence that I thought he was on the verge of decking somebody. He's capable of it, too—but he hasn't done it, to my knowledge, for years. He stays far away from liquor now, and he keeps himself out of situations that might provoke him—but still, he is hardly quick to forgive and forget. Late in 1975, we had the opportunity to book Barbra Steisand in connection with a film of hers, and everyone was looking forward to her appearance with a great deal of enthusiasm. Barbra had even promised to sing on the show—something she rarely agrees to do—and arrangements were progressing very nicely, with a lot of advance publicity and fanfare. Well, on the afternoon of the day of her scheduled appearance, someone representing her called up and canceled for her. It was an unbelievably rude and thoughtless thing to do, in my opinion—and apparently in Johnny's, too. He immediately went into a fit and remained angry throughout the entire taping. It showed, too—he said on the air how disappointed he was in Barbra for her lack of consideration and even reminded her that "The Tonight Show" had been instrumental in getting her career going when she was still moving from apartment to apartment and sleeping in foldaway beds in friends' living rooms.

The following night, Johnny managed to get some small amount of revenge in a characteristically tongue-in-cheek way: there is an actress named Madlyn Rhue, an occasional guest on the show and a friend of Johnny's, who was known for being able to do a marvelous imitation of Streisand. Johnny got her to come on the show to do her impersonation, and when the time came, out she oozed—wearing a typically tasteless Streisandesque dress, and outrageous Streisand hairdo, and enough nose putty to do the trick. After the laughter died down, Madlyn started to sing "People" in profile.

After about four bars, Johnny walked over to her and said, "I'm sorry—we're running out of time. Now get lost, Barbra."

In response to this, Madlyn feigned shock and huffed off the stage. The stunt may have been more than a little childish, but it did seem to get the demon off Johnny's back.

What Do You Mean, Johnny Isn't Hosting Tonight?

> People once said that nobody could ever follow Jack Paar. Now they're saying nobody can follow Johnny Carson. But don't you believe it. In this business, anybody's expendable.
>
> —JOHNNY CARSON

It seems to be the inexplicable rule that a larger percentage of bizarre and unexpected situations come up during guest-host periods than during Johnny's stints. I've often wondered if the guests who are scheduled in those periods don't sometimes subconsciously take advantage of what they know to be a tentative and not entirely stable atmosphere, much like children behave with a substitute teacher. In any case, guest hosts know the dangers and feel the responsibility, and they get ghastly cases of nerves before every show.

Each regular guest host tends to have a highly individualistic way of dealing with pre-show terror, and it's fascinating to watch their different styles being played out. The contrast between watching guest hosts prepare and watching Johnny prepare makes the spectacle seem even more extreme. In Johnny's case, it is a very low-key procedure—of course, it is also his show—but he has never seemed to need any elaborate pumping up, even, I'm told, in the early days. He has no entourage or agent or business manager floating around to tell him he's great or run interference for him, and the only enthusiasm pitch he gets is from Fred de Cordova, who does it as much for his own sake, I think, as for Johnny's. All Johnny really requires is a snack of a sandwich and coffee from the commissary and the efforts of his secretary to keep people away from him so he can work on the show. Some performers can't go to do a show unless they're covered by an entourage, like a security blanket. The entourage usually consists of agents and managers, but may also include hangers-on of all kinds—aging comedy writers, fair-weather friends, over-the-hill entertainers, groupies, hookers—you name it.

Joey Bishop is one of those who always seemed to have a whole raft of ancient comics and writers with him at all times. They'd carry his clothes, outdo each other with hack gags and one-liners, and just generally hang out. Sometimes I thought Joey kept them around just to have somebody to humiliate, since he frequently subjected them to "Who's the boss here?" fits and tantrums, particularly when there were other people watching.

Jerry Lewis had the weird habit, no doubt based on poverty in his youth, of bringing with him enough clothes to dress the entire city of Burbank. His retinue has been known to bring in literally 50 pairs of identically designed shoes, plus an entire wardrobe of suits, sportcoats, and shirts—all cut in the same Sy Devore style Jerry hasn't changed in some 25 years.

McLean Stevenson, on his hosting days, fluctuates between extremes. Sometimes he'll be a fanatic about having total solitude to sit and work on his material, and at other times you can't get him out from under-foot—he wants to use everybody as a test audience for what he's written. He used to spend the entire afternoon sitting in Joan Verzola's office trying to make her laugh, effectively keeping her from getting anything done in the way of work, and leaving her helpless.

By all odds, the most fascinating guy to watch preparing for a show is Don Rickles. He prepares his actual material only minimally—he never knows exactly what he's going to do or how—so for the rest of the time, he sits on a couch in his dressing room with the door open and, perspiring madly, proceeds to shout out something rude at every person who walks by. Since "The Tonight Show" studio is next door to the "Hollywood Squares" studio, Don also has an almost endless flow of fellow celebrities to tear to pieces, which of course delights him.

During guest-host stints, there have been a few times when Johnny's professionalism and smooth instincts for the show were sorely missed. The most memorable of them was years ago in New York when John Lennon and Paul McCartney had astounded us all by offering, through their attorney, to appear on the show. As I recall, they wanted to announce the formation of their new corporation, Apple, and while nobody could understand in the slightest why they would feel the need to promote it by coming on "The Tonight Show," we weren't about to blow it by telling them so.

The pre-interview was, as you can imagine, not held in the usual manner. They were at the peak of their popularity, having passed from mere teen-aged rock idols to universally recognized musical genies, and the security precautions that had to be taken for their appearance were taking up all my time. It was decided that they would be brought into the studio via a loading ramp which appeared to go into Radio City Music Hall, but which actually wound around subterraneanly and into the basement of the RCA building. They were brought up in an unobtrusive freight elevator under heavy N.Y.P.D. and internal security guard. They were then put in an out-of-the-way dressing room two floors above where the show was being taped, and they were, miraculously, never discovered there by fans. Teen-agers had been swarming out all the exits and entrances to the building since dawn, and all day we had been finding girls hidden on the sixth floor in dressing rooms and in closets and even behind water fountains—everywhere. We also had unbelievable problems with tickets for the show. People of major importance were calling up, one after the other, demanding tickets when the tickets were all long gone. I remember putting aside two tickets for Simon and Garfunkel, and when they arrived, they discovered that two people impersonating them had picked up their tickets and there was no way they could possibly get in.

When I finally got a chance to go up and talk to John and Paul before the show, I found that while Paul was easygoing and polite, John was, to use the archaic term, a wiseacre. The interview wasn't easy for me—in fact, I was freaked. How does one interview the biggest superstars in history at the apex of their glory without coming off like a boob? So I just punted; I went the direct route and tried to find out what, basically, they wanted to say to the audience and why they wanted to say it.

Apparently, the half-dozen or so questions I asked made sense to them, and after the last one—which I don't remember, but at which their eyebrows shot up —they said, "Now, who is this man who's going to interview us, this Joe Garagiola person?"

I told them who Joe was, all in the most laudatory terms, because I personally like Joe—but they had apparently already made up their minds that they didn't want Joe to interview them. What they wanted, to my horror, was for *me* to interview them! I spent five or ten minutes trying to explain to them that that was not possible, but it didn't sink in—at one point they even threatened not to do the show unless I would go on with them and do their interview. My life flashed before my eyes, I can tell you, because there was no way I was going to go out in front of that camera with the Beatles; not only would it have been a ridiculous condition upon which to end my tenure on "The Tonight Show," but I knew that it would also cripple my career permanently. Eventually, I talked them out of it and they agreed to go on.

But when they finally joined Joe, disaster struck. He started by asking one or two really silly questions and then went downhill from there. He just sat there saying things like, "Gee, I hope my kids get to see this," and, "Boy, am *I* going to be a popular guy in the neighborhood," *et cetera ad nauseum*. It was so inane that the Beatles became visibly uncomfortable, and Joe actually had to let them leave. The Beatles left believing that they had been sloughed off by this guy, and, in a way, I guess they had been.

But having a host excuse guests prematurely because he is overawed by their prominence is not an unusual occurrence. The one time that Steve McQueen appeared on "The Tonight Show," Johnny was so sensitive to him that he hurried through the interview and then quickly excused Steve, thinking that this was the most considerate way in which to treat such a shy man. Steve, on the other hand, had just started to settle down and feel comfortable about doing a talk show, and when Johnny said good-bye to him, he was hurt and dismayed and felt that he had let everyone down.

There is no way of knowing how egos are going to react; by fully catering to them, you frequently make them the most annoyed, but then sometimes, when they have been promised a quick "on and off," they will, if an interview drags out, feel taken advantage of. It's a very, very touchy area, particularly with people who designate themselves as superstars. In the case of the Beatles, however, there is no doubt in my mind that Johnny would have handled them well, and it's too bad that their only appearance on "The Tonight Show" was so shamefully botched.

I remember, too, some unfortunate and genuinely stupid highlights of their appearance. First of all, Tony Bennett had gotten out of a sickbed to bring his eight-year-old son to the studio to meet the Beatles. Because of security, he couldn't get near them before the taping. Waiting backstage for them to come off, security whisked them by before he could even say hello. Tony shrugged philosophically, and his son seemed thrilled enough just having been that close to the legends he considered far more important than his own father.

The day before their appearance I brought over their security director to NBC to meet with the head of our security. The Beatles' man was about six feet, three inches tall, distinguished looking in a blue three-piece suit, and, unusual for the times, had huge gray muttonchop whiskers. They discussed the routing for nearly an hour. Then when John and Paul were leaving from the underground garage, we were suddenly mobbed by kids who had somehow gotten in. So what did the head of security do? He grabbed the Englishman by the muttonchops and banged his head against the limousine! So effective was our head of security that he couldn't tell the difference between a man he'd spent an hour with the day before and a hundred screaming teen-agers!

On another occasion, a guest whom I was extremely anxious about, Charles Bronson, was slated to go on, with David Steinberg as guest host. The combination of those two really had me wringing my hands. If Bronson had ever done "The Tonight Show" before, it was in such a dim past that I couldn't recall it, and since we had this rare opportunity, I wanted the appearance to go flawlessly. As it happened, David's sort of open-ended flakiness paid off in a magical way and produced a side of Bronson that otherwise never would have been unearthed. The whole episode with Bronson was different from the very beginning; he is a very different sort of man.

Invariably, with a star of Bronson's caliber, it is almost impossible to get a working interview before the show. You can usually put together a skeletal interview based on press releases and magazine articles and so forth, but it will rarely have substance and *never* have depth. Therefore, I insisted that, in this case and for Bronson's sake, the publicist for the motion picture company arrange for me to talk with him directly. I remember that the appointment was at 1:00, and I had what was supposedly a home number. I say *supposedly* because normally the home numbers of stars aren't really home numbers at all—they're answering services.

Bob Newhart is a perfect example. You can have his "home" number, and when you call, you get the ubiquitous service, which in turn contacts his secretary, who in turn contacts him. In Bob's case, you can probably talk with him if he's not busy, because he is an extremely charming and affable man.

But in many instances with motion picture personalities—who are vastly more paranoid than television personalities—it's a comedy to try to get them in person on the phone. Therefore, when 1:00 rolled around, it was with a skeptical mind that I picked up the phone and dialed the number.

The voice at the other end said, "Yes?" And when I asked for Mr. Bronson, he said, "Speaking."

I was dumbfounded! Not only had he answered his own phone, but he had taken the trouble to be there at our appointed time. I managed to spend three or four minutes on the phone with him to establish some areas of mutual interest for his appearance, but I never quite recovered my composure while talking with him.

He showed up for "The Tonight Show" on time, not smiling—although smiling doesn't seem to be a characteristic of him—and was at all times extremely polite: "Yes, sir; no, sir; whatever you want."

He went on the show and David did the perfunctory interview that I had prepared, but somewhere along the line, David looked at him and said, "I get the feeling that you are *not* much of a liberal."

Bronson concurred.

David said, "Then you must not have thought much of my monologue."

Bronson said, without any reservation at all, "Yeah, I heard it. I didn't care for it much." And then he quietly drifted into a fascinating monologue about how he doesn't believe that reporters or, for that matter, writers in general can be trusted. He went on to say that he had attended many events in his life and that often when he read about them in the newspaper later, he had seen absolutely no resemblance to reality printed on the black-and-white page.

It was a riveting interview, once it got away from my gossip-column format, and David did a remarkable job. I suppose I am unhappy that Charles Bronson doesn't do more interviews, because the man obviously has a great deal to say. His early childhood years must have been grim. He grew up as part of a Polish, non-English-speaking family in a coal-mining town in Pennsylvania. He's not a big man—you expect him to be, because he exudes power much like Napoleon must have—in fact, he is well under six feet. He shared with me hideous recollections—like the fact that his family was unable even to buy clothes for their backs. He had to wear hand-me-downs in order to go to school—unfortunately, the hand-me-downs he got were from his sisters, so at that young age, he had to go to school in dresses.

Talking Jocks

For half a million I would wrestle Laurence Harvey nude in Times Square.

—JOHNNY CARSON

Occasionally a guest with immense appeal will not come directly from the ranks of show business but from peripheral areas. Most prominent among these are the sports personalities. For some reason that eludes me, some of these men tend to be, pound for pound, more impetuous and just plain off-the-wall than people who act out stories for a living. I think it's for that very reason that sports figures have always been an important feature of the show, and in fact, as we all know, there have been several athletes who have gone on to success as entertainers.

Among the many sports personalities who used "The Tonight Show" as a stepping stone to bigger and better things, the man who probably did it most successfully was Alex Karras. When I first met Karras, I already had something of a warm spot for him, since he had been an all-American at the University of Iowa when I lived in Sioux City. But I also knew everything that had ever been in print about him suggested he ate quarterbacks for dinner and slept with a Teddy bear, and I was even further encouraged by a picture I had seen on the cover of *Sports Illustrated* showing his pixieish face squooshed inside a Detroit Lions helmet; therefore, I booked him on the show.

Alex made his first appearance in July of 1970, and his entire demeanor in those days was that of an overgrown, pudgy little boy with thick glasses, ill-fitting clothes, and a serious, self-effacing manner. I remember in trying to prepare him for that first show, I was very worried about how he'd come off. But *Alex* wasn't; he kept assuring me everything would be fine and even seemed to have complete confidence in his showmanship. The pride was well founded. Alex started out talking about those instances in his football career which had been the most frightening for him, and the one he cited as the winner was having to take showers with the other team members in high school and knowing they were going to discover that he had absolutely no hair on his body. Alex always felt showers were the most frightening part of football.

Alex did considerable charity work in the Detroit area and at one time sponsored a celebrity golf tournament, the likes of which, I'm sure, the P.G.A. hopes never to see again. In place of the usual serious silence on the course, Alex had marching bands and mariachis and saw to it that a cannon would go off periodically in the middle of some golfer's backswing. He had a green with seven or eight different holes in it, and it was only by sheer luck that the players could figure out at which one they were supposed to shoot. Sometimes they had to shoot for all the cups in order to get in the one that counted. Then, too, another green might have no hole at all. He had left no stone unturned to distract the players and destroy their games. At the end of the tournament, he gave out door prizes. The man who was unfortunate enough to win first prize took possession of a car that could not be driven and which had to be towed away at a later date at the expense, naturally, of the lucky winner.

One remarkable thing about Karras was his total

candor about both himself and the world at large. He had been suspended in possibly the best season of his career—1963—by Pete Rozelle. Rozelle had bumped Alex and the "Golden Boy," Paul Hornung, for gambling. It could have gone much lighter on Alex, except that he admitted to the charge and even said, "What's wrong with it? I bet on my own team."

But Rozelle was unimpressed with his logic, and so for a year Karras was out of the business. He decided to do a little professional wrestling to pass the time. At one point, he and a professional wrestler named Dick the Bruiser were running a bar called the Lindell A. C. One of Alex's favorite tricks in the club (an incredibly tacky place frequented by hookers and cops) was to take a rookie up to one of the rooms, and while the kid was up there entertaining himself with a girl, all the rest of the people in the bar would go into the adjoining room and watch through a two-way mirror. One time, a fight broke out there, and when it was over, unbeknownst to Alex and Dick, six policemen had been badly roughed up and Karras was in hot water again.

Full-out was the way Alex functioned at all times, though you'd certainly never think of him as violent until you had personally seen him in action. There's a story Alex tells about what it's like to be in a huge stadium and be haunted by the voice of one person— one heckler out of 80,000—who for some reason has the pitch and the timbre that happens to perfectly suit a certain player's ear, and who can make every nasty comment heard all through a game.

The worst heckling place for Alex was Wrigley Stadium in Chicago. Every time they'd go in there to play, Alex could hear this one guy screaming, over and over, "Karras, you stink! Karras, you're shit! Karras, you're no goddamned good."

Finally, he couldn't stand it anymore. He knew exactly from where the voice was coming, and the minute the game was over, he went running up into the stands with blood in his nostrils. Everybody in the stands knew who he was gunning for, but when he reached his destination, what he found was a very small, frail Oriental man. The guy wasn't scared at all —he was only extremely flattered by the fact that Alex had bothered to come up there to kill him. Of course, Karras couldn't do it, and the man became a huge Karras fan as a result.

I remember in 1974, McLean Stevenson was guest-hosting "The Tonight Show" and reminded Alex of a time when they had met at a Rams game. At this game, McLean, Tim Conway, and Harvey Korman had decided to sneak into the game as mascots and somehow had gotten furry lion outfits to wear. Alex did remember the incident, and vividly, because he had been much more interested in the antics of those three fools than he was in the game. He also re-membered that Tim Conway had gotten hurt when a player crashed into him coming off the field, and Alex had been more than a little perturbed when the De-troit Lions' trainer had left an injured player in the middle of the game to go over to take care of this celebrity, this Conway.

If you were to ask Alex what his strongest recollec-tion of "The Tonight Show" was, I'm sure you would find it involved an encounter between his manager, Tom Vance, and Fred de Cordova. It was during a time when Alex had his own highly successful talk show in Detroit, a show which was only moderately football-oriented and killingly funny. Now, I had al-ways wondered why Alex had never guest-hosted "The Tonight Show." It seemed that his off-brand of kookiness would really work, but there were too many people with say in the choice of guest hosts (including Dave Tebet and the entire sales depart-ment) for me to be able to tell who was blocking the pass.

Tom, good manager that he is, was very anxious for Alex to host in those mid-years in 1973 to 1974, and he kept coming to me and saying, "Why can't I get Alex hosting? You know he should be doing it."

I kept saying, "I quite agree, but I simply don't have the leverage." I was fairly sure, however, that Fred would be susceptible to a frontal attack. Fred would say no to minions, but he was always reluctant to turn someone down to his face. Therefore, I said to Tom, "Why don't you approach Fred directly? I'm not getting anywhere."

So, at some point after the show, Tom took my advice. Afterward, he came into the dressing room all excited, and said to me—in front of Alex, in order to show that he was certainly out there doing his job for his client—"Well, Rudy and I had a long talk about Alex hosting and he didn't seem altogether negative."

I said, "Rudy?"

And he said, "Certainly. I was talking personally to Rudy Tellez, the producer."

Alex just looked at me and twisted his face into an expression of "Oh, my God, he did it again!"

I said, "Tom, Rudy *was* the producer. The producer now, the man you were addressing as Rudy, is Fred de Cordova."

Well, Tom went absolutely white and said, "Do you think that calling Fred 'Rudy' will affect Alex's chances of hosting the show?"

And I said, straight-faced, "No, but I think it will affect his chances of even *doing* the show again for roughly five to ten years."

The next great sports "comedian" discovery came from a most unusual source—Al Hirt's manager. One day he just called me and said, "Al tells me that he has a buddy who's a baseball player and is very funny." Well, that's the kind of third- or fourth-person recommendation to which you usually say, "Sure, sure," and which you then forget about immediately. But as it happened, I decided to meet with this man, a little-known baseball player, at the time, by the name of Bob Uecker. He works in a self-deprecating manner, much the way Alex does, but he seems to be able to create and develop more and funnier stories than Alex.

Bob played baseball professionally for 14 years (for everyone from Milwaukee to St. Louis, Philadelphia to Atlanta), and he *never* had any good years. Although he would never admit it publicly, Bob was a tremendously solid defensive player, but his batting average kept him in the bullpen. (He was also designated as a knuckleball catcher, which, of course, made his career much shorter than it might otherwise have been.) Bob made his first appearance on "The Tonight Show" in 1970, and Johnny kicked it off by quickly admitting that he didn't follow baseball and would have to ask Bob about some of the highlights of his career. Bob mentioned that he was proud to have set a lot of records. As a catcher, he had more passed balls in the major leagues than any other catcher at that time, and *he* hadn't played every day. He'd also been voted Comeback Player of the Year seven years in a row. He had been traded a lot and discussed the fact that they had always let him know in very subtle ways. For instance, after the game they'd put him on a plane to the wrong city. Or they'd send him on a U.S.O. goodwill tour to Vietnam—with a one-way ticket. Sometimes they'd stop him as he came off the field and the assistant manager would say to him, "I'm sorry, but there are no visitors allowed in the clubhouse."

Perhaps his most famous one-liner was in response to being asked how he handled the knuckleball. He said, "The best way to try to handle it is to wait until it stops rolling around; then pick it up and throw it to second base."

. He used to tell bizarre stories of what had happened to him in the minor leagues, coming up. He'd talk about how depressing it was to play in places like Idaho, where they wore used uniforms—places where there were no showers and they paid him $250 a month. The only thing that made it all worthwhile to Bob was the mad-hatter people with which he frequently had to deal. He remembered in particular one teammate named Rufus "Big Train" Johnson, an enormous black player who had thundering physical ability but not many I.Q. points to back it up. As usual in the minor leagues, the team often played night games in Podunk parks, and if the lights went out, it would take ten minutes for someone to get up, find the fuse box, and fix things. In the blackouts, Johnson used to do interesting things. For instance, if the lights went out and he was on first base, then he would be on second base by the time they'd come back on, thinking that no one would notice.

A wonderful example of Bob's insanity was a prank he pulled when he was with St. Louis. One of his close friends there was pitcher Bob Gibson, the brilliant Cy Young winner. When the official team photograph was taken, thousands were printed up and sent out for public relations purposes before anyone noticed that Bob Uecker was rather conspicuously holding Bob Gibson's hand in the front row.

One of Bob Uecker's unofficial team positions was as a "bench heckler." In a game where the manager thought that the umpire had made an error or was calling things in the other team's favor, he would put Bob on the bench next to him and would have Bob heckle the umpire. Of course, he would keep Uecker chattering away until he was finally thrown out of the game, but the coach didn't care, because Uecker was expendable. I think in one season, Bob was thrown out of more games than he actually played.

A story he always intended to tell on "The Tonight Show" but never got a chance to concerned manager Charlie Dressen, whom Uecker didn't care for at all. Dressen not only cowtowed incessantly to the press, but also had, in Bob's opinion, a very bad rapport with his players. Dressen also thought of himself as the greatest chili cook in the world, and he prided himself outlandishly on the slop he prepared. He never would share it with the players, which was a rather rude bit of egotism right there, and it always annoyed the team to have to watch this huge pot of chili cooking and to see the reporters who were giving them such a hard time on a bad day go over and be served a big bowl of it. Of course, the reporters would always say, "Gee, Charlie, this is great. This chili is fantastic," whether it was or not. So each of the players, when Charlie—or the press—was particularly rotten to them, always made a point of going by the pot two or three times a day and spitting in it. Their revenge would come on both Charlie and the press when they still heard the reporters saying, "Gee, Charlie, this is great chili," not even knowing the difference.

As it happens, it's the established sports stars—hoopla and publicity notwithstanding—who are not, I've found, all that thrilling as conversationalists. Football players like Franco Harris and Don Meredith are not too good in one-on-one conversation, even though Don happens to be a great counter-puncher, playing off a group situation, reacting to other people's stories and throwing in one-liners. I remember an incident with Don, though, that reminded me very effectively of the fact that, even if I wasn't necessarily dealing with the best talk-show guest in the world, I was still not exactly talking to the average Rube off the street. I had a dart board in my office that the staff would sometimes use to unwind before taping time. Once, as I was sitting in my office trying to get some good answers from Don for the interview and growing frustrated, Don got up, took the darts out of the dart board, walked to the back of the room, and in about eight seconds flat put five of the six darts into the bull's-eye. I renewed my efforts at the interview.

Of all the players in any sport who got bad-rapped and didn't deserve it, I consider Joe Namath number one on the list. I can remember once getting a limousine and going out to the airport late in the afternoon to pick up Joe from a flight and talking to him on the way to Shea Stadium, where the New York Jets training camp was based. LaGuardia Airport did not supply a bridge from the terminal to the plane—in other words, they pushed up a staircase and all the players had to walk down it. Almost all the other players had disembarked before Joe finally tried to get down. If the staircase had not had railings close together, he simply couldn't have *gotten* down by himself. Both of his knees were giving him such a hard time that it took him three or four times as long as it took a normal person to get down the stairs, and every step was obviously horribly painful. I never heard him complain.

Later, in the dressing room, when he was taping up his legs and trying to get ready—all the while kidding and having a good time—he asked Weeb Eubank, who was the coach at that time, if it would be all right if he altered his practice a bit to lay off the legs. Weeb readily agreed. I can remember walking through a deserted Shea Stadium with Joe and trying to find a concession stand open, since Joe's idea of breakfast in those days was two cans of Rheingold beer downed as quickly as possible.

Later, when Joe was appearing on the show, I slipped Johnny a card which said to ask Joe the question, "What kind of breakfast did you have?"

Well, Joe looked a little puzzled and said, "Oh, scrambled eggs, sausage, toast, I think—maybe some orange juice." And he went on to another subject.

I asked him later why he hadn't talked about having beer for breakfast, and he said, "Listen, I do have some private habits I'd just as soon keep private."

Joe was always one of my favorite people. One thing that helped was the fact that he had a sensational ability to remember names. I might not see him for 18 months or two years and he'd have little reason to remember me, and yet he'd still spot me instantly and call me by name. Joe seems to be a very private person, a man who is extremely loyal to his friends and who lives a life that's remarkably sedate. He's also absolutely and totally appealing to women of all ages—who invariably are treated by him with a great deal of warmth and respect, no matter who they are.

He did relate to me, in rather modest terms, that when he had casts on his legs after a collision with a charging linebacker and had to remain flat on his back for days, he was flabbergasted and flattered at the variety of ways his female companions had found to operate around and through his plaster casings.

There was a song years ago which claimed, "You've Got to Be a Football Hero to Make a Hit with the Beautiful Girls," and it seems to hold a great deal of truth to this day. Burt Reynolds used to hang out, as a moderately unknown actor, with the Dallas Cowboys, sitting on the bench in total obscurity and accompanying the players to various social events. At one of these road parties, Don Meredith said to him, with a gleam in his eye, "Tonight I'll be Burt Reynolds and you be Don Meredith." So, sure enough, when they went into the party, Burt was introduced to everybody as Don Meredith, the football player, and he said he never had so much sexual action in his life—not before, and not even since as Burt Reynolds, superstar.

In terms of fascinating personalities in sports, golfers seem to be the one exception to the rule. They seem to be dull to a man, with the single—and stellar—exception of Lee Trevino. I remember Lee being asked once how he pronounces his name. He said, "East of the Mississippi, where they like Italians, I pronounce it 'vino'—like wine. West of the Mississippi, where there's more Mexican influence, I pronounce it 'vinyo.' The truth is, I don't give a damn one way or the other."

Lee is a far cry from the polished, country-club types you usually find in the golf world; he never had a chance to go to college, let alone join a country club. He just caddied, he said, for centuries. Lee considered himself a terrific caddy, mainly because he worked barefoot. He had prehensile toes and found he could make much better tips if the player he was caddying for could see that Lee was improving the lie of the ball by massaging the grass around it with those toes. Lee actually may be the best golf hustler who ever lived. He used to tell me stories about his caddying days as a kid in El Paso. He and his pals, when they'd get bored playing the same old 18 holes over and over, would invent new courses. For instance, they would tee off at the normal place, but then play to the green on the ninth hole, instead of the second. Or they would hit balls from parking lot to parking lot all through downtown El Paso or create a course consisting of tunnels, culverts, trestles, buildings, and so on. If a housewife was foolish enough to leave her doors open, Lee would play right through her house. For three years, Lee played golf only with a taped-up, quart-sized Dr Pepper bottle, a tool with which he claimed he could beat everybody—and did, provided it was on a short course.

Lee's stature as a tournament golfer faded for a couple of years, and when I asked him what he thought accounted for that, he said, "It was the lightning." He is referring to the incident on June 27, 1975, when he and Bobby Nichols and Jerry Heard were all struck by lightning during the second round of the Western Open in Chicago. Before that disaster, among the three of them they had won 34 tournaments. Then for several years, only one had won a tournament. Lee had back surgery, Heard was ill, and Bobby Nichols didn't win enough prize money to pay his caddy. The interesting part is that although none of them seemed to be physically injured, the lightning apparently affected their central nervous systems and they haven't been quite right since. Lee says that for a guy who's never been afraid of anything, it sure bothers him that now even a flashbulb popping can shake him up enough to put him off a stroke.

Authors and Thieves

> I don't know where the boys get their love of show business. My husband and I are both retiring and conservative.
>
> —MRS. HOMER CARSON
> [Johnny's mother]

Needless to say, not all of my favorite characters and stories come out of the world of sports. What may be the most profound practical joke in my experience was the work of a man not usually associated with rollicking humor—William Peter Blatty, author of *The Exorcist*. Bill was a frequent guest on the show even long before *The Exorcist* was published. Bill is second-generation Armenian—his parents literally arrived in America on a cattle boat—and his mother supported the family by selling homemade quince jelly. They never had rent money, so the family moved every three months throughout Bill's childhood.

Bill is a very quiet and polite man but with an absolutely riveting look. He is dark and Arab looking but with steely gray eyes, which he claims are the result of a Crusader slipping into his great-great-great-grandmother's tent. He's the type who loves to tell stories—especially to one person at a time—and when he fixes you with those cold gray eyes, you listen.

Well, at one time, before Bill achieved substantial fame, a friend of his persuaded him that he could pass for an Arab sheikh in the Beverly Hills circuit, and Bill, hopeless prankster that he is, decided to see if it would work. From somewhere in a studio wardrobe, he got a gown and a desert headdress, and after adding dark glasses and a haughty demeanor, the two of them started going out in a leased Rolls-Royce to "in" cocktail parties. They saw to it that the story leaked out that Bill was a star-struck Saudi Arabian prince with an incredible amount of money, and it soon became the "thing" to have this guy at your parties—in fact, if he wouldn't come to your party, it was deemed a failure and you were a social albatross. Naturally, Bill started being invited to smaller and more intimate gatherings and his sense of humor almost exposed him more than once. He was invited one evening to the home of Dick Powell and June Allison, who were highly impressed by his royal status. (If actors and actresses are indeed the royalty of the United States, then, believe me, they are twice as awed as the rest of us by authentic royalty.) Throughout the dinner, which was really a family gathering, Bill sat and nodded and looked very solemn, but he couldn't resist putting them on. When the salad arrived, he began eating it with his hands, much to the horror of the Allison-Powell family—but they recovered quickly and then, if you can believe it, they put aside *their* forks and began eating *their* salads with their hands, just to make sure they wouldn't offend the "prince."

Eventually, Bill let the story get around that he was approaching a time when he was going to distribute a portion of his fabulous wealth to whomever had befriended him most, and of course the flurry of parties increased. Then one night when he and his friend were at the Brown Derby—a favorite haunt of the sheikh's and packed with the wealthy and famous—Bill got up, rattled off a stream of pseudo-Arabic words, and tossed a handful of fake "jewels" across the floor. Of course, all these Beverly Hills "sophisticates" immediately dropped to the floor and began clawing at each other over these little pieces of plastic, and on that note, Bill swept out of the restaurant never again to appear in that persona.

Another of my favorite moments was created by David Steinberg at a party I was hosting. David came with a group of very nice people and proceeded, as is his wont, to get quite drunk simply on the atmosphere. David rarely partakes of stimulants—he maintains that he is able to get as wrecked as the most wrecked person at a party simply by osmosis. At one point in the party, he came up to me and said, "Craig, isn't that Sandy Baron over there?"

To which I replied, "Yes, David, it is Sandy Baron."

And David said, "You know, Craig, I've never been able to stand Sandy Baron, and I'm afraid that if he says hello to me, I'll have to leave."

Well, unlike David, I had partaken *eagerly* of stimulant and was, in fact, quite tight by that time—so David's statement sounded perfectly reasonable to me. I simply smiled and said, "Of course, David. Absolutely."

Suddenly, David wheeled and yelled across the room, *"Hello, Sandy Baron!"*

And Sandy, of course, yelled back, *"Hello, David!"*

Whereupon David turned to me and said, "Good night, Craig," and left the party.

An interesting phenomenon I found in this work is that some of the best performers—also some of the smartest and most interesting guys—are the ones who are not the best schooled, in a formal sense. A perfect example of that is Sammy Davis, Jr., who was raised in show business and whose school was "the road" and who can't, the story goes, read or write particularly well.

One "regular guy"—the man I liked best of all I met during my tenure and whom I most wished I knew better—is Joseph Wambaugh, the former policeman who has authored such books as *The New Centurions, The Blue Knight, The Onion Field,* and *The Choir Boys.* When I first met him, he was just coming off the glow of his first best seller and was still an active member of the L.A. Police Department. He is a man of great candor and always has fascinating stories to tell about his work, but his overlying attitude is always love for the streets and the people on them. "The Tonight Show" actually had a big effect on Joe, not to mention the other way around. Through guesting, he met author Truman Capote, and it was Truman, on a weekend with Joe and his wife in Palm Springs, who convinced Joe to write the book that was most difficult for him, *The Onion Field.*

Another time, Joe met Dave Toma on the show and the two of them—Joe from Southern California, who thinks of himself as a "sub-cop," and Dave from New Jersey, who's considered a "super-cop"—became fast friends. They even, at one time, shared an agent, so how close is that?

The fascinating thing about Joe is that he didn't think highly of himself as a cop. I remember him once being asked on the show if he didn't think his badge, nightstick, and gun were all extensions of his masculinity. Joe thought about that for a minute, and then said, "God, I hope not—I'm so bad at handling all three." When really pinned down on why, with his obviously high intellect and his insight into human nature, he had never progressed in his twelve years on the force beyond the rank of detective sergeant, Joe responded that he had frozen himself on purpose; he did not want to leave the street and become an administrator.

One time, Johnny got Joe into a discussion of groupies. When confronted, off the cuff, Joe admitted that, like performers, policemen did have groupies. I think he shocked a great many people when he explained that a surprisingly high percentage of American women need a father image, and if they never had a good one, they compensate by making themselves sexually available to another authority figure—the policeman. Years after this revelation, that thesis became the theme of his book *The Choir Boys*. *The Choir Boys* is a rather erotic book which has been compared favorably with other investigatory works like *Catch 22* and the motion picture *M*A*S*H*. When one reads the book, one should remember that every single word of it is true—except that the names have been changed to protect the not-exactly innocent. Every incident in the book is drawn from experience, including the part about the commander who made love to his secretary on his desk and lost his toupee every time she had an orgasm.

Joe seems to have a wonderful relationship with his wife, but it must have been strained at different times; he was an active participant in "choir practice," which is code for those times when Joe's wife would *really* have wanted him home. On several different occasions he was interviewed in bars of marginal repute, which he seemed to love to frequent, and he used to spend a considerable amount of his off-time in a police bar in San Gabriel where the waitresses work bottomless. The bar is owned by an ex-cop and is called The Other Ball. Something about these bars seems to hold a perverse appeal for cops; in fact, the time in his life Joe told me that he felt most threatened—and fascinated—was in Chicago in a cop bar that was full of every conceivable kind of sexual and physical deviant, from transvestites to dwarfs. He said he felt more nervous there than he did during the Watts riots, but he also went back more than once. I think that Wambaugh's ready access to "The Tonight Show" was not a thing that endeared him to his superiors—especially to Ed Davis, the notorious police chief who spent many hours and plenty of public money trying to worm his way onto the show to express personal points of view.

Without doubt the most interesting—and sometimes difficult—people I worked with as a class were the comics. My strongest recollection of meeting a new comedy act was in 1971, when I had my first encounter with Lily Tomlin. She was a virtual unknown at that time. She came into my office rather shyly and was extremely polite and careful with her words. I finally said, "Well, may I see what kind of material you do?"

She said very demurely, "Well, yes. . . ." And then she got up and began to do a pantomime. It was remarkable, of course. She played a girl going into one of those twenty-five-cent photography booths found in bus stations and five-and-ten's. The girl carefully put in her quarter, and then she began to pose. On the first picture she smiled shyly; on the second the smile was a little more aggressive; on the third it was almost a leer; and on the fourth frame, she lifted her skirt up over her head and flashed the photo box. I knew right then that Lily was too wonderfully weird to pass up.

One comic about whom I've always felt very ambivalent, with whom I've had both very good and bad experiences, is Bill Cosby. Bill changes from moment to moment—you never know where you stand with him. I've seen him come on "The Tonight Show" completely unprepared and yet work himself into a monologue which is warm, original, and killingly funny. At other times, he's been cold and aloof, maddeningly playing the superstar, and even talking down to the audience. I remember once going over to the Burbank studios, where he was shooting his series, to talk to him about an appearance he was going to make on "The Tonight Show." I found him in his bungalow, upstairs over the dressing rooms, with a cook who was preparing enough lunch for about a dozen people. To anyone who happened to walk by, whether or not Bill had ever set eyes on him before, he would call, "Hey, man—come on in and have some lunch." But to me he was totally and inexplicably rude, pushing me aside as if I were not there, ignoring my questions, failing even to offer me a seat, let alone any of the food that was being handed around. It was not as if we were strangers, and his behavior was hard to take.

His mood was so bizarre, in fact, that I had real misgivings about his appearance that night. Still, he was the star and I was the coordinator, and so I tried to be professional and ignore the rebuff. When he actually *did* bomb that night, I couldn't enjoy the revenge, because I knew his lack of control would probably jeopardize his value as a talk-show guest, and he was, in general, just too good to lose.

Now the flip side of Bill is this: the next time we wanted him to do the show, I got hold of him and said, "Listen, I've got an idea. The Harlem Globetrotters are doing the show tonight. Why don't you come over? We'll find a uniform for you and we won't even announce you—we'll just have you out there with them doing their opening routine to 'Sweet Georgia Brown'—we'll let the audience discover you there."

Being a former Temple University basketball player himself, Bill loved the idea, and he came into my office before the show, saying, "Okay, where do we get the uniforms?" and rubbing his hands together.

We went poking around, and in one of the smaller dressing rooms we found a box containing all the uniforms. Bill was like a kid in a candy store.

He hissed, "I'm going to steal a whole set of these." And then he proceeded to grab the shirt, shorts, socks, warm-ups—everything—and tuck them under his arm. Then he turned to me and said, "Okay, now we've got to find a set for *you*."

I said, "Are you kidding?"

And Bill said, "So, okay, just take this shirt."

To my surprise, I did. That shirt is still sensational to wear on the beach when I want to look like a fool —it's a size 50 long and hits me about mid-ankle, which really impresses the girls.

One special problem I've found with comics is the practice—a very common one—of flat-out stealing another's material. It has always shocked me. Many times a young comic would come to audition, and out of his mouth would come, word for word, a routine that wasn't just written by, but was strongly *associated* with another comic. At first, I didn't know how to handle that, but eventually I grew sufficiently callous to rattle off the who, what, when, where, and how of the comic from whom he stole the piece. Sometimes, it wouldn't even faze him, and then I'd get downright brutal.

I remember a comic who shall remain nameless (and who probably will, period) who gave his coordinator a set of fully plagiarized notes. He was sitting in makeup before the show, and I happened to walk in just as the production assistant was handing him a contract to sign. I said, "Don't you think you should also add the names of David Brenner, Robert Klein, and David Steinberg to that?"

And he said, "Why?"

I replied, "I think that since you're doing their acts, it would only be fair to give them credit on the contract."

He just shrugged—he didn't care who knew.

Some comics actually felt insulted if they were called on their thievery, although I've never understood why. One of my closest friends in the business is a sensitive and amazingly realistic personal manager named Buddy Morra, who handles some exceptionally original talents like Robert Klein, David Letterman, Robin Williams, and Martin Mull.

Buddy and I went down one night to a club in Greenwich Village to see a music act he was thinking of representing, and as we were sitting there with the 11 or 12 other people in the club, the emcee, named Carl Waxman, came out. Now, Carl was once more famous for "borrowing" material than for being truly funny, so we knew what to expect. We watched and, sure enough, right in the middle of his routine, with Buddy sitting in the audience, Carl went straight into a Robert Klein piece—a piece that could not have been even *remotely* associated with anybody else.

Buddy finally couldn't stand anymore and interrupted from the audience: "Carl, don't do that, all right?"

Carl shot back: "Well, now—wait a minute. How long has Bob been doing this particular material?"

And Buddy said, "Oh, for about five years, Carl."

At that point, Carl became incensed, retorted with what he imagined was a perfect piece of logic—he said, smugly, "Well, I've been doing it for two!" Somehow, to Carl, that made it all right—as if five years had put it in the public domain.

Still, Buddy had gotten Carl flustered, and he did abandon the Klein material—but the clincher was yet to come: Carl didn't retreat to using his own material; he turned right around and dissolved into Woody Allen material, (Woody is another client of Buddy's office), even to the point of scratching the top of his head and hunching over like Woody does. It was fascinating to watch, and with that, Buddy just shook his head and gave up.

The youngest comedian ever to appear on "The Tonight Show" was a kid by the name of Alan Bursky, who later became an agent (until the head of the agency caught him performing again and fired him). When Alan was first booked, he was only 18, and he looked much younger even than *that*. His initial appearance was good—partly because of his youth and partly because of some genuine talent—but there was one story in particular that stands out in my mind. Alan was joking about having moved from New York City straight into a residential motel in a tacky suburb of Los Angeles. Like many New Yorkers, Alan just hated California—he felt it was the final jumping-off place for human sanity. But the thing that offended him more profoundly than anything else was the palm tree. Alan is of the opinion that the palm tree holds first, second, and third places in the "World's Most Ugly Tree Contest," and it was to his chagrin that in California, it isn't enough that they plant them—at night, they have to put multicolored lights on them so you can see them 24 hours a day.

While Alan's first appearance was fine, his second

and third were not so good, and unlike some comedians whose careers blossom from one or two clever "Tonight Show" performances, Alan's appearances seemed to dampen his career, which was quite odd. Alan also had a problem in that he annoyed the key clique of comedians, headed by David Brenner and Steve Landesberg, who, in their own way, have a great deal of power. Alan ignored their distaste for him and used to try to join their tables at the different places comedians and performers hang out in the wee hours to drink and lie. Usually David and Steve would flatly tell Alan to go sit someplace else—and they really claimed to have found him detestable, though I sometimes thought it was much more a matter of good show than reality.

Brenner does like to tell, however, about the time he was invited to a cocktail party and was read the guest list as an inducement. The story goes, apocryphally, that there was a long string of fascinating celebrity names, but at the end, the host mentioned Adolf Hitler, Idi Amin, and Alan Bursky—at which point David supposedly cried, "Not Alan Bursky!"

Second Banana
and First Trumpet

There are some nights when he's very
lackadaisical, when he just doesn't want to
get started. Those are the nights I'm needed.

—ED MCMAHON

Two of the people I have so far put off discussing
happen to be the two people on whom Johnny Carson
most depends on the air—Ed McMahon and Doc
Severinsen.

Johnny's relationships with these men are highly
complex—in fact, the men themselves are highly complex, no matter how light they are made out to be for
the audience's sake.

Johnny's relationship with Ed is probably the most
revealing, since they have been working closely together for over 20 years, know one another like books,
and bounce off of each other with an almost auto-
matic precision. Many people wonder just what Ed's
function is on "The Tonight Show," and that's a
complicated question to answer. I've heard a lot of re-
sentment from outsiders who think that Ed makes
barrels of money for doing nothing more than saying,
"Heeere's Johnny!," laughing at the monologue, and

then sitting through the show. It ain't so. Still, his role is so subtle that even he and Johnny occasionally have trouble pinning it down. I remember that once when they had been doing the show for seven or eight years, Johnny came into Ed's dressing room after the show's anniversary party in a very nostalgic and even tearful condition.

He blurted, "Ed, I know what you do for me—I know what you're doing on the show." And then, overcome with emotion, Johnny left the room.

Ed turned to me and wondered out loud, "What *is* it I do on the show?"

One of the things he does is function as a foil for Johnny—much like the hapless member of the audience Don Rickles needs to bounce jokes off. Ed, of course, is a highly skilled announcer and a major personality in his own right, but what he does with Johnny is, in its way, as fascinating as what Dean Martin did with Jerry Lewis in their heyday. Everyone kept saying that Martin couldn't possibly get along without Lewis if they broke up, and I'm sure people think the same of McMahon and Carson.

One of Ed's chief responsibilities, of course, is to prepare the audience—to warm them up for Johnny's monologue. Once he's done that, he makes the opening announcements and then plays off Johnny's monologue, laughing either when he thinks something is funny or when he thinks Johnny has to be rescued from a joke that just died. He then comments on Johnny's clothing or goes into any given situation. For example, if the monologue isn't going well and Ed knows Johnny wants to get off with a laugh, Ed will, rather than walking over to Johnny with the prop for the first commercial—say, a Budweiser bottle—toss it from off-camera to him, so that Johnny can either happen to "miss" it, or can fumble with it until it falls and breaks. Johnny, thereby gets a big laugh to exit from the monologue, and everybody is happy.

The most difficult and critical period of the show for Ed is that part in which he and Johnny sit down after the monologue and the first commercial. At that point, Ed has to carefully study Johnny to find out exactly where he wants to go, and what he wants Ed to do or to set up for him. Sometimes Ed's instincts don't work exactly right, as with one awful instance I can recall in which Ed was trying to anticipate where Johnny was going with a joke and did *too* good a job. Johnny was reading from a newspaper article, doing a rather lengthy setup based on the premise that scientists had found that people who were very sexy were exceptionally vulnerable to mosquito bites. Now, Ed, without thinking, went for a laugh by slapping at his own hand and was having a great old time with the audience when he noticed that Johnny was shooting daggers at him. Ed had, of course, haplessly stepped all over the joke that Johnny had elaborately set up for himself (even to the point of having behind the desk a can of insect repellent), and Ed knew right then that if he had been anybody else, it would have marked his last time on the show.

Another of Ed's primary functions is to say things about Johnny that Johnny himself can't say—comments on his clothes, compliments, mentions of what Johnny did the night before, or how he was received in his Las Vegas act—setups that will let Johnny do a joke on himself.

Ed and Johnny look after each other a bit in their private lives, too, although there are periodic cold spells when the competition between the two of them gets particularly heated or when they both get into a jealous, self-protective stance about their stardom. Nevertheless, they will probably continue to hang out together for many more years to come. I remember a story about Johnny's between-marriage bachelor days in New York, when he was still drinking and used to get pretty lost after a party or a night on the town. On one of those nights, Johnny ended up spending the night in Ed's apartment, sleeping on the living room couch. Very early the next morning, waking up in a strange place, forgetting where exactly he was and thinking he heard someone at the door, he walked out into the hall to look up and down, and the wind blew the door closed behind him. There he stood, locked out in the hallway in his jockey shorts, beating on the door and yelling, which, of course, Ed couldn't hear, being tucked away in a back bedroom fast asleep in a Budweiser dream. Johnny had to stand outside beating on the door and waiting literally for what seemed like hours, and when Ed finally went to the door, not knowing what had happened, he found Johnny in such a rage that he was nearly sobbing.

The audience and "The Tonight Show" fans have a very strange reaction to Ed. For example, he seems to attract a certain kind of highly aggressive female, and he gets a lot of neurotic letters from all over the country which say things like, "I know you were in Dallas last night, and you didn't call me. You have to stay with me; how dare you?"—when, of course, he wasn't even in Dallas and certainly doesn't know the writer from Adam. Lots of demented love threatens like that.

Then I have seen him literally assaulted in the parking lot by people wanting autographs. But Ed, even though he is often clearly distracted and in a hurry to get somewhere, is never anything but completely gracious and courteous, and, in fact, rarely turns down one of those special autographs or pictures that people on the NBC tours love to take back home and talk about forever. I've been with him a couple of times in restaurants when he was quietly eating his dinner, and a perfect stranger—sometimes even a whole family of them—would walk over, pull out a chair, and just sit down to talk. What's more, they would take liberties and make remarks, for which I was ready to belt them—even though they weren't talking to me—but Ed seems to have an absolutely endless tolerance for them. He says that because he is, in a sense, in their homes every night, they somehow feel he's a member of the family, and they treat him accordingly.

Actually, if Ed has any cross to bear, it's the fact that he has acquired this reputation as a drinker, and that myth being reinforced both by his size and his ruddy complexion (not to mention his identification with Budweiser), most of the public believes that he gets juiced every single night. Of course, it isn't true. In recent years, Ed has become one of the "white wine" people—*i.e.,* he drinks socially and neatly. In fact, now, virtually all of Ed's drinking has been directly related to social activities—especially dinners —and he certainly is not the kind of man who has a bottle in that second desk drawer and nips at it all day long.

It must be admitted that Ed has been known, on occasion, to drink to excess, but then who hasn't? At a couple of my parties, for example, he has managed to relax and get sloshed, but it's good for him to unwind like that, in my opinion. Still, he's extremely conscientious about not driving after he's had a few drinks, and there's always a driver waiting for him outside a restaurant or party.

All in all, Ed is the kind of man with whom you wouldn't mind hanging out. He's gregarious, warm, and extremely intelligent. What's more, he's a great storyteller, and who can resist *that?* Another quality that endears him to others is that he's not very impressed with his own celebrity status. He rarely uses his influence as a personality to get an edge he wouldn't otherwise have. In fact, he usually bends over backward the other way, even when it concerns something as relatively insignificant as obtaining a better table at a restaurant.

Ed did get himself in trouble once by being too trusting and probably even too ambitious. It was in connection with a traveling show that he and a friend put together during the Bicentennial, a show designed to demonstrate, on behalf of the Teamsters Union, the contributions that trucking had made to the United States over the years. He and his partner took the profits made from this show and bankrolled a film that was to be made in Israel. Unfortunately, the movie turned out to be a turkey—but meanwhile, the Teamsters Union was busy manhandling the traveling show. It was so popular with the union guys that, instead of letting the show move on after a day or two as scheduled, the city's local union heavy would call up headquarters and say, "I'm keeping the show a couple of weeks over, see?" Eventually, it got so thick with the union that some muckraking journalist got hold of it and decided that Ed McMahon was in collusion with the Teamsters—with all the "syndicate" connotations *that* involves—and that he was, in fact, taking so much money from them that he could afford to finance overseas films with it. In fact, the reporter went on to suggest that maybe the Teamsters, with Ed's help, were financing the films for some sinister reasons of their own. On and on, of course, the whole thing deteriorated into a court case which was inevitably dropped, but Ed's good name was sullied, by the inference alone, for several years.

If Ed McMahon is as easygoing as they come, Doc Severinsen is, in spite of his "loose" on-camera demeanor, just about as intense as they come. Doc is possibly the hardest person to read, with the exception of Johnny, on the entire "Tonight Show" staff. His talent and musical ability are obvious, and his wit and charm are also there for anybody to see, but in his own way, he is as closed as his boss. He is actually reluctant to *speak* more often than not. I sometimes think when it comes to talking, he is a little self-conscious about his lack of a college degree, but the fact is, he is worldly far beyond anything formal education could have taught him.

Doc has been Johnny's conductor for over ten years, but he had been with the band many, many years before reaching that position. He was a trumpet player in the back row when Skitch Henderson was conductor, and when Henderson was succeeded by Milton DeLugg, now the conductor of "The Gong Show," Doc began to move up. But Skitch used to feature

Doc for a particularly evil bit of business. When the show was still an hour and forty-five minutes long, the first 15 minutes in many markets consisted of Skitch and Ed doing some music and some chat before the show got rolling. (Before that, of course, the first 15 minutes involved Johnny—but when he found out that many markets didn't pick *up* the first fifteen minutes, Johnny refused to come on the air until that time had passed.) Anyway, that first 15 minutes was something of a showcase for Skitch and his band. Now, if someone like Al Hirt was going to be a guest on the show, Skitch would see to it that Doc was featured in a number in the first 15 minutes so that everyone would realize that Al Hirt was, in fact, not really a superior musician to a member of Skitch Henderson's band.

Finally, when it was decided that Milton DeLugg and his accordion were not quite right for "The Tonight Show," Doc was sent off to conducting school and there got his first taste of real music study outside of a band bus in the Midwest.

Johnny and Doc have always gotten along fine, but they're not close friends—in other words, if there was a problem with one, he wouldn't first go to the other one to help work it out. They don't socialize much except on sort of semi-business occasions, because Doc, like Johnny, is very much a homebody, a loner who basically hates parties.

Doc doesn't drink at all these days, but he used to—and constantly. He started out in bands at a very young age, and being on the road with traditional "boozing and doping" band types, he learned to follow along with whatever they did. He quit drinking one day, cold turkey, under rather unusual circumstances. He had been over at some friends' house for dinner and had been drinking the whole evening.

Afterward, one of the friends took a deep breath and said to him, "Doc, we think you're an alcoholic."

And he said, "Don't make me mad. I can take the stuff or leave it."

To this they replied, "But you seem to be taking it all the time."

Doc kept on insisting it wasn't a problem, and the three friends got into a bit of a fight.

When he was driving back home, Doc automatically felt like he needed a drink and stopped and bought a six-pack to get him the rest of the way home. Someplace along the way he said, "Wait a minute—they may be right. If I had to get a six-pack to get me home, then I do have a problem," and at that moment he tossed the six-pack and determined never to drink again. He apparently hasn't had a drink since, and I certainly take my hat off to him for that. The man has strong will and strong character. On the other hand, you know that anybody capable of extremes like that also can carry around a few idiosyncrasies—maybe even weaknesses.

Doc's dressing room, which was admittedly small and unattractive, always reminded me of what a garage sale would resemble if it were hit by a tornado. It was a catch-all—outrageous clothes scattered here and there, record albums, opened mail, unopened mail, and posters of various products he endorses, ranging from earphones to LP preservatives. There would be a carton of his latest LP's (unopened), trumpet mutes of varying sizes, pencils with no points, copies of *Downbeat* and *Playboy*—the full catastrophe. It certainly looked lived in, but not necessarily by humans. Ed's office, in contrast, was always extremely neat, though it was completely filled with Budweiser and McMahon memorabilia like photographs, awards, and trophies. The impression one got from Doc's office was that this might be his last week on the show and he didn't want to get too attached to anything around him.

Doc's habit of leaving mail unopened is an especially interesting one. When the show was based in New York, Doc always insisted that NBC should have a secretary for him. I can remember sitting in on a conversation between Doc and Rudy Tellez and hearing Doc say, "You've got to get me a secretary."

To this Rudy replied, "It's not in the budget."

Doc came back: "Ed has a secretary."

And Rudy retorted, "He pays for that secretary himself." The secretary later moved to the West Coast with Ed, experienced her first earthquake, and instantly moved back to New York, but at this point, she was a bone of contention to Doc.

He kept saying to Rudy, "It's not for me to open my mail and take care of all those things."

So Rudy finally said, "Come on, let's go into your office."

They went down to Doc's tiny office at the end of the hall—an area not much more than five by six feet —and there were the notorious stacks of unopened mail. Rudy turned to Doc and said, "Do you mind if I open a few of these?"

And Doc said, "Go right ahead."

Rudy must have opened about a dozen envelopes, and he found that at least three of them were offers for work which said things like, "I've got ten thousand dollars if you can do one night in Atlantic City," but of course they were all outdated by that time. Rudy said, "All you'd have to do is open your mail and play two of these gigs on a weekend and you'd make more than paying a secretary for an entire year."

To that Doc replied, "It's the principle of the thing."

Although Rudy was losing patience, he carefully said, "The principle is that it's costing you a fortune not to be paying a secretary to take care of your own business."

Doc just said, "I'd rather lose the money than pay for her myself." Doc's stubbornness was not well known, but it was deep-rooted, nonetheless.

I think it's fair to say that Doc is recognized as the best technical trumpet player working anyplace in the world today. Either he is only a technician or his technical prowess has concealed his soulfulness, but the fact is, he isn't a man who regularly produces hit singles. Part of it is his inability to be categorized musically, but Doc isn't willing to compromise on that point. For example, he got into a rage once when he was out on the road doing a concert and a crusty old music professor in a bad tweed coat with cigarette ashes on it kept asking Doc why he didn't play standards like "Green Dolphin Street." Doc said it infuriated him that a man who knows the history of jazz would want him to play only for a small minority of aficionados, when Doc was trying to reach and please a great range of people. He was angered just as much by the music editor of a college newspaper who insisted that Doc should only play jazz versions of current rock-and-roll tunes.

Actually, Doc is not a man who is deeply disgruntled with his life, but he may wake up occasionally and say to himself, "How in the hell did Herb Alpert or Chuck Mangione sell all those records?," or "God, if I could only get one good, solid hit." Somehow, he's always been just a little late. Even a highly respected musician like Sammy Davis has had the experience of getting onto a tune later than everyone else and having some moderate success with it, but never quite getting the jump for that big killer record of his own.

When Doc got into the position of music director, he repeatedly made it clear that he wanted nothing to do with selecting talent. Nevertheless, he would constantly be stopped by people and be asked why he couldn't book them on the show if he was indeed in charge of music. He always felt a bit ambivalent about that. If he actually suggested someone, they were always considered, of course, but he never wanted to be put in a position professionally of vouching for them. Doc and I used to get great pleasure, in my early days, out of managing to get an act on against everyone else's will and then watching them go on to become a big hit. In fact, two of the people Doc was influential in helping me get on the show early in my career were Richie Havens and Melanie. For some reason, Doc also seemed to be the one who people who couldn't get on "The Tonight Show" always approached with a

"Why does Johnny hate me?" or a "Why can't I get on the show?"

Of course, he'd tell them something like, "Hey, man, I don't know anything about it—I'm just a horn tooter." But it was a tough spot for Doc to be in because he is usually a soft touch.

Another cross Doc always had to bear was putting up with the unprofessionalism of young musicians: the overnight-hit groups who'd come in without their music —or, worse, without even being able to read music— or who'd be late, or whose accompanist (the one insisted on) would get lost on the freeway and fail to show up. Doc felt responsible for all the music on the show, and so an unprofessional attitude literally infuriated him, although he'd usually keep his feelings to himself. I can remember some years ago booking a well-known rock-and-roll act, the Youngbloods, who had made it very clear they were merely condescending to be on "The Tonight Show" when they came into the studio for rehearsal. They immediately started bitching that they didn't like the acoustics, and they didn't like the lighting, and they didn't like the set that had been designed for them, and they didn't like the microphones, and they didn't like this, and they didn't like that.

Well, as it happened, Johnny was watching all these antics on the monitor up in his office. He came immediately downstairs, walked into the studio, and said, "Okay, boys—wipe your noses and go on home."

Doc's glee at that was remarkable—it was a tangible thing, even though he admitted to me later that the group had unquestionably sold more records than he ever had.

(Dick Carson once endeared himself to the talent coordinators during a taping with another fly-by-night rock group. After Dick had carefully blocked their two numbers in rehearsal, they totally changed their presentation for the actual taping, making Dick's shot selection look amateurish. So for their second number, Dick never once shot any of the performers, only the set. And what did the rock-and-rollers think? They thought it was "Groovy, man!")

Doc's outrageous clothes, once a regular feature of the show, started with one wild tie. The tie got such a response that it gradually developed into a whole wardrobe syndrome that he was forced to maintain and that cost him more money than he'd like to admit. He even started to wear slightly wild-eyed clothes on the street, and I know his outlandishness has been a big influence on fashion, serving as encouragement for men to go ahead and be peacocks if they have a mind to do so.

Doc's real name is Carl. His father had been a dentist, and as a child, Doc was called, "Little Doc," later shortened to just "Doc." Doc has been married three times. I don't know much about his first wife, but his second wife was an extremely attractive and articulate woman named Yvonne. They grew up in the same part of Oregon and had been childhood sweethearts, but both went on and married other people. Years later, both divorced, they found each other again and got married. Yvonne is a strong, very personable woman, but rather domineering, I believe. She has a great deal of money; she's reputed to own something like one out of every three trees growing in the state of Oregon. At the time "The Tonight Show" moved from East to West, I know Doc went through a definite trauma with his marriage. Yvonne more or less stayed back East and there was a gradual disintegration of the relationship. Whether that was mutual or not is not my question to ask. In any case, after twelve years of marriage, Yvonne sued for divorce on the grounds that Doc had deserted her, and the judge apparently agreed; she was awarded $75,000 a year in alimony, a couple of cars, and the Severinsen's farm in New Jersey. She probably would have gotten more if it were not for her own personal wealth.

For many years Emily Marshall was secretary and assistant to producer Fred de Cordova. I had met Emily years before, when we both had lived on the same floor of a slum apartment building on Prince Street in Greenwich Village. I remember once coming home from NBC and finding I couldn't get into my one-room apartment because the entrance to the building was blocked by a movie crew. When I asked the assistant director why they were using this specific building, he answered, "Because after weeks of searching, the art director decided this was the ugliest building in New York." Years later, when Emily joined the show in Burbank, we renewed our friendship. I was extremely pleased to hear that Emily had tired of her job with Fred and started writing for television. Her first script was good enough to get her a job as a story editor and she has since written for many of the most successful sitcoms. On May 17, 1980, following a rocky courtship, Emily and Doc were married at his home in Hollywood in a private ceremony.

Doc recognizes that "The Tonight Show" has made him a highly, highly visible musician—he is, year after year, voted the number-one band leader and trumpet player in the United States by such magazines as *Downbeat* and *Playboy,* whose accolades he attributes to a lucky position on "The Tonight Show." He thinks of his years with the show as sort of his golden era—but, if you ask him if he is the best leader and trumpet player in the United States, he just laughs and shakes his head derisively. He undoubtedly underrates his own ability. Doc always says that when "The Tonight Show" ends for him, he'll be just as happy packing it up, maybe doing shows in Las Vegas, doing an occasional tour, and cutting more records. He refuses to get attached—or at least admit to it.

...And My Staff
Shall Comfort Me

> The reason [Carson] didn't have a whole lot
> of close friends was because he was a little
> preoccupied with his profession. He just
> didn't take time.
>
> —JERRY SOLOMON,
> Fraternity brother

The most interesting thing about these two men, Ed
and Doc, in their relationships to Johnny is that they
both keep a low profile; they are aware of the dangers
if they stick their heads up too far on "Johnny's Show."
That's a fine line to walk—the difference between
being an addition to the show and upstaging Johnny
—and even when they try their best, it doesn't necessarily work. For example, I once asked Joanna
Carson what she thought of Ed's relationship with
Johnny. She said, to my surprise, that it was a love/
hate relationship. She thought that actually Ed hated
Johnny in some ways and was extremely jealous of
him, even though he knows they are good for each
other and even though they have been together for all
these years. What was more surprising to me was to
find out later that that jealousy goes both ways.

I think that at times Johnny even becomes a bit jealous of Doc's celebrity status. I've heard him say more than once, "Damn it, does Doc have to dress so outrageously? He looks foolish!" When he says that, he's really reacting, in my opinion, to his fear that Doc may be distracting from his own stardom and high profile within the realm of the show. Most people also find it a bit curious that Johnny hasn't really ever had Doc in his Las Vegas act. Actually, it's right in character. Fortunately, Doc is not a pushy person, and any ego problems that arise with Johnny seem to be smoothed out instantly. Doc is aware of Johnny's needs, and he's willing to simply do his best to contribute to the show on whatever level he might be needed.

Johnny's penchant for surrounding himself with professional "Number 2 men" who won't rock his boat is carried over even into his choice of directors. That's not really surprising; the director performs a very personal function for the star and has to be in his camp all the way. For years, Johnny's director was his brother, Dick. When Dick went on to other things, Johnny hired Bobby Quinn, whose style Johnny likes. Johnny likes his style mainly because Bobby knows what's important—and what's important is that Johnny be the center of attention, the focus of the camera action on "The Tonight Show." It won't do to have the audience hear just his voice, because what he's *saying* is only half of what counts. Johnny's real stock in trade is an expressive face, and if the camera doesn't pick up his sight gags, he's dead. So, if Johnny comes right out and says to Bobby, "I don't have enough close-ups," Bobby will simply nod and give him more of them. It is that inherent *ability* of Bobby's that I think has earned him Johnny's adamant loyalty.

Working for Johnny in any capacity is an unsettling position in which to be. Among those who have worked for him on the show, Johnny has a reputation for being a cold fish—clinical, fanatical about performance, even tyrannical—but with no corresponding friendliness, even in relaxed moments, to soften the blows. Personally, I didn't agree. Being a Midwesterner, I'm burdened with a similar reserve to Johnny's, and I can promise you that during the years I lived in Iowa, no two people who couldn't stand each other ever smiled through their Yves St. Laurent caps and said, "Let's have lunch." But Johnny was *never* actually cruel or brutal, so I tended not to take his coldness as a personal affront. But, on the whole, as a boss, his emotional limitations are a problem. For one thing, the pressure on the show is tremendous; people are working themselves into apoplexy five days a week, and basically they're doing it to make Johnny look good. When he seems not to give a damn about their extra efforts, it smarts.

Obviously, he's difficult to know—and the reticence doesn't diminish, no matter how long you've worked for him. At first glance, he seems to be warm and gregarious, but if you make the mistake of thinking you can pursue that line of warmth, you will run almost immediately into a shallow barrier beyond which there is simply no going—ever. He is a perfectionist, so the consciousness is there that you must at all times strain to do your best work. On the other hand, I found that specificity of Johnny's vastly preferable to working for someone who vacillates—who doesn't know what he wants. But perhaps the most unsettling facet of Johnny's personality, especially from the employee's point of view, was his inability to confront people on the staff, face to face, about anything negative. You'd hear of his displeasure second- or third-hand, or not at all, and so you never knew if he loathed you or loved you. He also had a terrible time firing people, and since he always hedged about it, rumors were constantly circulating that he was planning to fire this or that staff member—including, at one time or another, Ed, Doc, Fred, and all their predecessors. You simply knew he wouldn't give you any warning to your face, so it was like living with an axe poised and ready to fall on your head. It was contractually easier for him to fire the writers and producers, and I often think that's why there was such a high turnover with them. When Johnny wanted a writer or producer fired, he only had to wait until the man's 13- or 26-week contract had expired, and then instruct the business affairs people not to renew it. It was as simple and bloodless as that.

Domestic Crisis

> It's strange how there are always plenty of
> agents and managers around when you're
> working but not when you really need them.
>
> —JOHNNY CARSON

At one time, early in his career, Johnny was being represented by the management team of Bruno and Shields, and he always believed that they were selling him out or trying to replace him at NBC with another of their clients, Mike Douglas. He heard more and more evidence to confirm this notion, and he finally fired them. Unfortunately, they went on collecting, contractually, a huge amount of commission from him —it added up to something like $400,000—and that rankled Johnny even more.

After I left "The Tonight Show," I was contacted by Westinghouse Broadcasting and was flown to Philadelphia to see if I would like to take over as producer of "The Mike Douglas Show." I spent two or three days there and decided it wasn't exactly what I wanted to do, but I did have several nice conversations with Mike. Mike, of course, knew my background with Carson, and once during lunch, he said to me, "You've got to tell Johnny something for me. The truth is, I really tried to help him back when he was having problems with Bruno and Shields."

He was referring to the time Johnny had contacted him directly and said, "I know you know the truth about all this—would you give a deposition? And would you make sure it gets to court on time? Because it will make or break me against these guys."

Mike told me that he did, in fact, go out and give a deposition, but for some reason, that document never got to court. When I asked Mike what had happened to it, he said, "Well, knowing the character of some of the people involved in the case . . ."—he shrugged and continued—". . . I'd say something changed hands that made the piece of paper disappear." He said, "I know Johnny's never forgiven me for the whole episode, but still, I really did try to help him with that case."

Johnny also loved to badmouth the William Morris Agency, which had represented him for a time—very badly, he thought. His ire probably had to do with the fact that on his opening night at the first big club date he had ever gotten, the William Morris people never even bothered to show up, which he felt was not only indecent, but also a shirking of their obligations to him. They always treated him like a second-rate personality, and he always hated them for it.

Then there are the domestics. Because of the size of their home—and because of their station, of course —Johnny and Joanna have live-in servants. They've had nothing but problems keeping them. Partly, it's Johnny's aversion to having strangers in his private sanctuary (in the same way that he doesn't want a chauffeur knowing his business), and partly it's also plain bad luck. For some reason, the couples available for hire always seem to look old and dead—but worse, they are always flaky in some way that's not immediately obvious.

The Carsons once had a man who lasted only a few days because he insisted that not only should he eat a bit better than the Carsons, but that, out of necessity, of course, he should consume at least one bottle of the Carson's best wine with each meal, including breakfast. He was a German from the old school, and he basically felt that he was due equal privileges to Carson himself. He was the type who clicked his heels and bullied the rest of the staff, particularly the housekeeper, who was a Hungarian woman. He really despised her, but only because she was from Hungary. The trouble with this particular domestic started in earnest one day when Johnny was arriving home from Las Vegas. He got to the house exhausted with a car full of dirty clothes and a burning desire to put his feet up to rest. He called for the German servant to help him unload the car but was informed that he was in Beverly Hills getting a haircut. The next time Johnny asked for his assistance, he was told that the fellow was at the movies. Well, at that point the servant had been employed for only a few days, and Johnny figured if he was like that during the first week, what would he be like after he got to feeling at home? The thought of that sent Johnny into a rage. In fact, he got so angry as the night wore on that he decided to wait up for the German to come home from the movies, which he didn't do until the wee hours of the morning. Joanna remembers waking up in the middle of the night and hearing this terrible fight going on down in the kitchen. When she finally ventured downstairs, there were the two of them, standing in the middle of the kitchen in their shorts, screaming at each other. The German was blaming everything on the housekeeper because she was Hungarian—exactly the kind of bigotry that drives Johnny up the wall—and so Johnny said, "You're leaving this house right now!"

The servant replied, incredulously, "You can't throw me out in the middle of the night!"

Johnny came back: "Oh, yeah? You just watch me!"

And on and on they went until the German said, "You really believe that Hungarian, don't you? How can you believe her? Hungarians don't remember anything."

Johnny yelled back, "They remembered *you,* you son-of-a-bitch—*you invaded their country!*"

And then, of course, it turned into a free-for-all. Nevertheless, when dawn broke, the wayward domestic was indeed out on the street, with only his German luggage for company.

Then there was a male employee whom I shall call "Henry." Henry decided to quit one Saturday morning while Johnny and Joanna were in Las Vegas, and so he just left—leaving the house unattended and the property unguarded. When Johnny got back and found that this man was so irresponsible that he would put Johnny's home in jeopardy on a whim, he went berserk and refused to pay Henry the week's salary he claimed he was owed. Joanna is sure Henry will one day drag them into court demanding that week's salary and about 15 years' worth of back interest at 12 percent—and she's probably right.

But wait—there were others. One couple that came to them highly recommended—by the de Cordovas, if memory serves me—looked like they were going to be perfect, at least for the first few days. But then Johnny and Joanna came downstairs one morning and found the couple in the kitchen, absolutely falling-down drunk. Well, unfortunately, ever since Johnny's successful battle to quit his drinking habit, he's been a maniac about anyone else's heavy drinking, but especially if it involved someone in his own household. (Joanna doesn't drink much, however.) When he saw those servants drunk, he cracked. He called a cab. He told the two they had five minutes to get packed, and boom!—they were gone without a trace within a quarter of an hour. While Johnny supervised their hasty retreat, Joanna left to take her son, Timmy, to school. When she got back, she walked into the kitchen and found Johnny mopping the floor, stark naked except for a peasant bandanna on his head. Joanna told me later, "I just laughed until I cried. He's a very funny and a very sensitive man."

Off Duty

I lived in a building for six and a half years and didn't know my next door neighbor's name. I liked it that way.

I'm not going to sit around in a roomful of people pretending to have a good time and saying, "Oh, isn't this fun?", when it isn't. I think it's a waste of time doing something you don't really want to do because people think you ought to.

—JOHNNY CARSON

This may sound eerie, but I firmly believe that no one—including Johnny's own family—really knows him intimately. The Johnny Carson who's seen around town a bit, who goes to an occasional party, who socializes only rarely, is actually more reserved, formal, and unreadable than the man you see in your home for 90 minutes a night.

That doesn't mean that Johnny doesn't get along with people; actually, he fits easily into any environment and seems at home with any sort of group, from upper-echelon, Beverly Hills "society" to beer-drinking poker buddies. He has a license plate on his Mercedes which reads "360 GUY," and most of us believe that he ordered the plate to subtly tell the world that he considers himself an all-around human being. But Johnny, when confronted with that, gets terribly irate and says he had nothing to do with the plate, that it came that way in the mail. It *is* possible Joanna ordered it for him, because I know he surprised her with her personalized plates, reading "BABE"—Johnny's nickname for her for many years.

The behavior Johnny adopts at parties can be rather bizarre. It was much more so when he was an occasional drinker, but he is still unpredictable and strange at times, an effect which I think is not altogether unintentional. Sometimes he will come to parties unannounced, make a few odd remarks, and then leave just as unexpectedly as he arrived. It's as if he's taunting everyone with his unavailability, his inscrutability—but what I really believe he's doing is making certain he'll have center stage, even after he leaves. The funny thing is that he doesn't have to worry.

Perhaps the most bizarre experience I had with Johnny Carson was early in my career, when I had been on the show for only about 18 months and was striving to get closer to the show's hierarchy in order to create a better position for promotion. Little did I know. Anyway, Dick Carson, Johnny's brother, was leaving his job as director of "The Tonight Show" for a job in California as director of the first Don Rickles show—which, like virtually all of its successors, was a failure. Come to think of it, anything would feel like a failure compared to directorial duties on "The Tonight Show," but apparently Dick needed to prove he could make his own way, without the "help" of his superstar brother.

Johnny decided to throw Dick a going-away party at Danny's Hideaway, a nefarious steakhouse in New York where the famous and near-famous hung out, and where they could even be served dishes named in their honor (like the "Fat Jack Leonard" baked potato). Johnny scheduled the party for one of the private rooms upstairs so that we could all honor Dick in uninhibited style. Early in the evening, standing beside Johnny, I thought to ingratiate myself to him by mentioning that we had grown up in the same part of the Midwest—Iowa. He couldn't have cared less. In fact, to my chagrin, he gave me the old "So what?" brush. As the evening progressed, Johnny got more and more depressed, thinking about his brother's leaving, and as his misery increased, so did his alcohol intake.

At that time, he was not what anyone could possibly call a happy drinker. About halfway through the party, for no apparent reason, he came over to me and said, "If you ever get into a fight, here's what you should do." And with that he demonstrated, in three quick moves, how he could pull out my eyeballs, smash my testicles, and rupture my diaphragm before I could even get my hand up to defend myself. It frightened me not a little to know that if he was steamed enough, rationally or not, he could physically destroy anyone, regardless of size or age.

As the evening progressed, people began to disappear and it was obvious to all of us that the empty room was in large part attributable to Johnny's behavior. He had, I remember, a roaring fight with Shirley Wood that night, but no one except Shirley seemed to be concerned, since they knew Johnny would have no recollection—or no *active* recollection —of his tirade the next day. Firings and hirings in party contexts were, therefore, meaningless and shrugged off by everyone.

As the night wore down, I, being still in my starstruck state, hung out to watch Johnny, and ended up as one of the last dogs to be hung. At that point, John Carsey, wanting to protect Johnny's reputation and his own job, suggested that Johnny wanted to leave, and why didn't I go with him to make sure he was well taken care of? Well, that plan had mixed appeal to me. It was terrific to be "hanging out" with Johnny Carson, not to mention being flattered by having the associate producer say, "You take care of him—I trust you." I realized, on my way down to get a cab for us, that Johnny had turned the corner. Fact was, he was visibly high and I was responsible for him.

I immediately thought, "What do I do with this man? Do I take him back to the U.N. Plaza, where he lives and where he obviously doesn't want to go? No. Then where should we head from Danny's?" I didn't want him hanging around the bar area at the entrance of Danny's, where he'd be seen, even though he could be forgiven for getting drunk, considering the occasion. so finally, with some help from John Carsey, I managed to get him into a cab, whereupon he immediately decided he wanted to go to "Jilly's" place.

Now, "Jilly's" is a notorious bar on the West Side of New York. It's named after Jilly Rizzo, an infamous associate of Frank Sinatra's and a man for whom Frank apparently feels unbounded loyalty and devotion. Frank even sends his own people to do Jilly's errands and delivers special guests to his bar. Nevertheless, on that evening I was not too thrilled to hear that Johnny wanted to go to Jilly's—it was not the ideal place to be found by the trade columnists.

Fortunately, I had landed a cab with a hip black driver, and when he opened the divider a slit for instructions, I leaned forward and said quietly, "Take us to Jilly's—the *long* way, please." He glanced over his shoulder and assessed Mr. Carson's condition and just nodded. Well, we must have driven around Central Park two or three times and had been traveling for 45 minutes when Carson suddenly realized that we had been driving an awfully long time and still hadn't managed to get from Grand Central Station to the near West Side. It normally should have taken two or three minutes. He started to bitch at the driver. Well, since I had put the driver up to it, I felt rather defensive and said, "Uh, there was a lot of street construction— it's taking a bit longer than usual and the theaters are letting out and there is heavy traffic"—and so on with a gaggle of flat-out lies.

Finally, after at least an hour of stalling, we got to Jilly's. We went inside, sat down at a tacky little table, and each of us ordered a drink. Johnny's arrival caused no stir at all, and he didn't try to make one; he had sobered up from the ride. A few drinking buddies and acquaintances wandered over to the table and Johnny talked pleasantly to them all.

Finally, late in the evening, Johnny looked over at me and said, "Kid, go on home. I know you've got better things to do than hang around here." And he threw in a lascivious wink to intimate, I suppose, that I should go home and get laid.

So, leaving him in the hands of Frank Derone, the house singer, I reluctantly disappeared with no assurance that I would have a job to go back to tomorrow. Characteristically, Johnny never said a word about it later, but I regarded it as probably the key moment in a long study of how close you should allow yourself to get to the man in charge—*i.e.*, not close, not close *at all*.

I believe my favorite Carson drinking anecdote concerns, coincidentally, a party that he attended at my house. When the show was based in New York, I lived in a very centrally located area on Fifty-fifth Street between Fifth and Sixth Avenues, and each Christmas season I would host a well-attended bash known in the annals as the "Artillery Punch Party." It became moderately notorious in its time, as I always managed with a couple of cups of artillery punch to make a splendid number of people totally blind for days afterward. As it happened, a friend of mine, not associated with "The Tonight Show," had invited some friends of his, and one of them made a rude pass at Charlotte Clish, Johnny's secretary at the time. Charlotte was highly offended, belted the guy, and then got slapped in the face herself. (There was, needless to say, a lot of heavy drinking going on.) I went over and apologized to the fellow for having to ask him to leave, and to my relief, he left, grudgingly.

A while later, Johnny decided it was time to go home. Now, he was in fairly decent shape and in a great mood, but Charlotte, for some reason, decided that *she* had to take care of *him*. Johnny got up to leave and started asking everyone where he had parked his car. Of course, no one had the vaguest idea. There were two parking lots on my street, but he swore he hadn't left it in either of them, that he had left it on the street. I volunteered to go out and find the car, but he waved a hand, saying, "No, no, no," and he and Charlotte went waltzing out into the early morning air. I must say I was a little worried about him driving himself, especially with Charlotte along. I envisioned them both winding up in the police tank and, amid scandal, me knocking on doors at "The Merv Griffin Show."

The following day, I went into work and, hearing nothing detrimental, crossed my fingers that he'd gotten Charlotte home and that there were still such things as miracles. I stopped Charlotte later in the hall and tentatively said, "How did it go? Did he find the car?"

And she said, "It was right there on the street. We didn't have any problem."

I said, "What about driving? Hadn't he been drinking a little too much to be driving?"

And Charlotte said, "Oh, yeah, he had had a lot to drink, but he was extremely careful, the way he maneuvered his car down Fifth Avenue."

I said, "What do you mean, careful?"

She said, "Well, he stopped at every traffic light—regardless of what color it was."

Of course today, the drinking stories are a thing of the distant past.

I think that one of the reasons Johnny doesn't go to too many parties is that he can't relax at them; it's as if every social situation is for him a competitive arena, and he can't quite put his self-image aside. I'm not talking about "flashing"—a popular sport in Beverly Hills in which all conversations are limited subtle indications of this success or that purchase—I'm just saying that for Johnny, social gatherings are experienced more like sports events. The question for him is:

"Who is the most physically and mentally able?" And if that game isn't already going, he'll kick it off.

Johnny likes to play cards, also, and while he doesn't really have time to study card games, he plays them with great intensity. Johnny's best game-playing buddy, Bud Robinson, takes a lot of abuse if Johnny loses, but he doesn't seem to mind.

Bud also plays a game which drives Johnny up the wall, a game called "Categories." It is relatively simple: everyone takes a piece of paper and draws 25 boxes, five down by five across. Atop each of the five columns, the players write in pre-agreed categories—let's say, "Movies," "Cars," "Book Titles," "Plants," "Food." Then the group chooses a five-letter word—say, "Party"—and one letter of the word is written outside of each of the five boxes on the lefthand side. Finally, operating under a time limit, each player has to place a word in each box that starts with the corresponding letter and also describes an object that fits with that column's category. The most original word for a given category wins the most points. Well, Bud always used to win at that game, and Johnny would always come in second. It made him furious. He liked to think he was more intelligent than Bud, and the fact that he was unable to beat Bud at this dumb game got him really steamed. In fact, Joanna hates to see them start a game, because whenever Johnny loses—which is most of the time—he broods about it for days afterward, and she has to suffer it.

In Me I Trust

***

Put it this way—we're not Italian. Nobody in our family ever says what they really think or feel to anyone else.

—DICK CARSON

Johnny has always had plenty of trouble deciding who his friends are. He never knows in his own mind who likes him and who doesn't; who is genuinely concerned about him and who just wants to use him. He believes he's in too powerful a position to be able to trust even his fellow entertainers—his peers, the people who could really lighten his load.

But there are other people in the world besides entertainers, and not many of *them* have made the grade, either. As Ed McMahon says, "Johnny is not overly outgoing or affectionate. He doesn't give friendship easily—or need it."

Friendship, to Johnny, is not a matter of the unfettered giving of people with like minds, as it is to most of the rest of us. He describes it like this: "By a friend, I mean someone who you can talk to about your views on philosophy, religion, *et cetera,* and know that that's as far as it will go—somebody you can be open with." In other words, he means primarily a client-lawyer or patient-doctor relationship. The main

213

criterion for friends is that they have large ears and a sealed mouth.

Johnny will call his interpersonal attitude "guarded" or "private" or he will say he's just minding his own business, but there is more to it than that. A quote that appeared in the *Los Angeles TV Times* not long ago reveals a bit of his slightly persecuted feelings on the subject of his fellowman: "They call me a loner. It's like you're damned if you do and damned if you don't. If you go out to parties, you're a bum and a rounder; if you stay home and live a quiet life, you're a loner—a snob. There's a strange fetish people have of rooting for the underdog on his way up, but once he gets there, they want to knock him off—they throw rocks at him. It goes with the territory."

Now, the idea that if Johnny and Joanna did more than the meager socializing they now do that Johnny would be termed a "rounder" is a bit extreme. The truth is, the man is shy and basically uncomfortable with other human beings, and he squirms under close personal contact. True, there have been plenty of incidents that have helped speed him along the path of anti-humanism, as there have been with most public personalities. Theirs can be an intolerable life. Johnny remembers that one time when he was standing at a urinal, his hands obviously occupied, a man actually came up and asked him for an autograph. Johnny, disgusted, turned on the man and said, "And just what would you like me to sign it with?"

We're Not
the Nelson Family

Looking back is kind of a silly thing to do.
I don't look back that often.

—JOHNNY CARSON

Joanna Carson is an extremely attractive woman; in fact, it would be difficult to imagine how any man could fail to be attracted to her. She has clear, green eyes, is tall and slender—a former model—and always seems to be well tanned, well tailored, and thoroughly poised. She has the elegance of a woman whom you just know will age with grace and beauty.

But you can guess that Johnny Carson is by no means an easy man with whom to live. Although he seems to have a need to be married all the time, he has reputedly never been totally open with any of his wives. He is not an overly generous man; he doesn't give Joanna many gifts, unless it's to repair a fight or make up for pushing her too far. But this is in direct contradiction to the verifiable fact that he recently bought Joanna an $80,000 Rolls-Royce. On top of that, she has to contend with Johnny's competitive temperament. If Johnny loses a tennis game in the morning, for example, he may not speak to Joanna—who, of course, had nothing to do with it—for the rest of the day. All in all, he is not the textbook ideal of a good husband.

There seems to be a real barrier between Johnny and his family. More than just a prickliness, it comes down to Johnny on one side, the rest on the other. The two factions don't even talk much unless it's called for, and they certainly aren't closely knit. Joanna's job, at times, is to be Johnny's official wife and to cater to his every whim, and that's what she does. She is also charged with being at all times loyal and close-mouthed, which she is to a fault. Joanna is really a very warm person—also much more hip than Johnny—and it must be difficult to pay the price she does for that coveted position as the wife of Johnny Carson. She is, of course, never anything but laudatory of him both publicly and privately, and she has my respect for that. (But then as a life-long bachelor without the courage to let anyone stay close to me either physically or mentally, I can't criticize those who do.)

Joanna was previously married to a man named Tim Holland, a handsome fellow who is reputed to be the finest backgammon player in the world and who, in fact, makes his living at it. Joanna met—if that's the correct word—her present husband shortly after her divorce, when she was on a date at a Manhattan restaurant. Johnny was sitting at a table nearby and, obviously taken with her looks, began a hilarious flirtation routine to catch her attention. He would do things like miss his food with his fork or miss his mouth with his fork—a lot of stunts which were charmingly juvenile.

Although the yellow journalists are constantly trying to catch Johnny in an adulterous situation—*i.e.*, printing blurbs in their gossip columns along the lines of "What noted talk-show host was recently seen in the Polo Lounge with two hookers?"—it's been clear from Johnny's behavior that he's been a frustrating target and only vulnerable to innuendo. Between marriages, he was not that careful; he was a bachelor. Johnny has a strong sexual bent, and while it is certainly acceptable for us civilians, it causes him to act with caution. Sammy Cahn told me once about a night in New York in the mid-sixties when he was walking along a Manhattan street on his way to P. J. Clarke's. In the middle of the street was a character dressed in full hippie regalia—beads, long hair, fringed jacket, boots—walking along with girls on either arm. Just as Sammy was saying to himself, "Jeez," and shaking his head, the character called out, "Hey, Sammy—dont go away. Don't you recognize me?" It was Johnny Carson. He was laughing like a fool. He didn't want Joe Public to recognize him, but he had enough of a macho streak to want his buddies to know what he was up to doing.

Prior to his marriage to Joanna, Johnny was married for many years to a woman named Joanne. (The fact that all the women in his life have had names that start with the letter "J"—like first wife Jody; then Joanne; and now Joanna—is probably pure coincidence, but it's *odd* coincidence. Or it may be pure pragmatism, because in this way he doesn't have to get new monogrammed towels each time.) Joanne, also a pretty brunette, was an actress of marginal creditability, but she was also probably the most devout Johnny Carson fan who ever walked. In fact, Fred de Cordova claims that even in the period during and after the divorce—which was instigated by Johnny and which was singularly unpleasant because he wanted his problems kept private—Joanne continued to speak of Johnny only in the most glowing terms. She was, nevertheless, a little off center, and her flaky, repudiatedly ludicrous behavior was a source of irritation and embarrassment to Johnny.

It was around the time of this divorce that "The Tonight Show" was scheduled to move to the West Coast, and finding out about the plan, Joanne moved herself to Los Angeles in advance. The fact that she was there in town waiting for Johnny when he was expecting to have a fresh start on the Coast perturbed him immensely, and part of his annoyance was undoubtedly due to the fact that her presence there would fan the divorce-gossip fires and sap off some of the good publicity he had hoped to generate by moving the show West.

To give you an indication of how gullible "Hollywood" is, Joanne, who had very little theatrical background and whose "career" had really been as a stewardess, managed to put together a résumé which made it look like she had in-depth theatrical and on-air experience. After hiring herself a publicist, she was able to parlay a non-existent career into an actual, if undistinguished, one. At one point, her name was appearing in the trade papers almost every day. She'd even be linked in items with some of Johnny's best friends, like Truman Capote, and that was really absurd. The publicist always managed to find something to write about her, and indeed, she did appear in print more frequently than any other member of "The Tonight Show" ménage, which irritated Johnny to no end. Ironically, she wound up with her own rather silly television talk show called the "VIP'S," which was mercifully short-lived.

Johnny's first marriage, and the one that produced his three sons, was to a girl named Jody Wolcott—an extremely attractive blonde who has scrupulously shied away from the limelight, and who now lives happily on a farm in upstate Connecticut.

Joanna seems to be very fond of the three boys, especially the older two, Chris, 29, and Corey, 26. She thinks they have matured nicely and, what's more, that they are surprisingly unaffected, non-materialistic, for having been raised in an environment where there was always increasing wealth and fame.

On the other hand, according to Joanna, Ricky, the 24-year-old, can be a problem. She finds him more materialistic, more competitive and resentful with Johnny, and also very emotionally high-charged. Ricky was the only one of the boys who ever considered changing his last name, although why he thought a common name like Carson could brand him for life, I don't know. Joanna thinks he made the move just to subconsciously get at Johnny—not really as a rejection so much as a manifestation of a conflict: his desperate wish to actually *be* Johnny and his inability to live with those feelings. Ricky had problems growing up. He had trouble in school, he had trouble with teachers and other kids—he even got arrested several times, usually in conjunction with some driving offense that also involved an overindulgence of artificial stimulants. The only time in his life that he seemed to have it together was when he went into the navy. He became a photographer and got shipped off to one of the poles, and let's face it, there just wasn't much of an opportunity there for him to run amok.

Actually, most of Ricky's problems may center around the fact that, of the three boys, he is the most *like* Johnny and is therefore least able to cope with the highly competitive atmosphere that Johnny, by his nature, has set up for his sons. There is no way Ricky can really hope to emulate his father's success—and there is also no way he feels he can really hope to please Johnny.

Ricky now works on "The Tomorrow Show"—away from Johnny, where he can feel more his own person, and apparently his growing pains are disappearing.

The only one of the boys I had any real personal contact with is Corey, the middle one. Corey worked on "The Tonight Show" for a while as an assistant to the assistant conductor, Shelly Cohen. It was Shelly's job to keep the band and all the music organized for Doc, and he gave Corey a job that was invented for Morgan Mason, son of Pamela and James—a job that amounted to being a "musical gofer." Corey is a quiet, very witty young man who, like his father, keeps to himself and takes some getting to know. The fact that he worked on the show did not mean that he hung around "Dad's office"—he, again like his father, is not the sort to take much of an interest in family goings-on, whether they're at home, at the office, or wherever.

Although he worked for only about a year at his job, Corey took his work seriously and was conscientious. I'm sure he made almost no money, but he, nevertheless, lived alone and on his own resources. He was grateful for the job mainly because it was music-oriented, and Corey aspired to being a musician. In fact, he went on to study guitar in college. He didn't care if it was rock, flamenco, or classical—he just wanted to be the best of his kind, whatever that turned out to be.

As for Chris, the oldest—he graduated from college with a degree in psychology but had never really gotten his life organized. He planned, for a while, to be a professional golfer and played in a few tournaments in Florida, but is basically a teaching pro.

As with Joanna and Tim, Johnny's relationship to his boys is not exactly an intimate one. It's the same even with Johnny and his parents and, to a lesser extent, with his brother, Dick, the one family member of whom Johnny truly seems to be fond. Johnny Carson is not a family man in the true sense of the word—rather, he is, in a very real way, in the world alone.

Johnny and Dick were raised in an upright Methodist family, and while they seemed to come away with none of the religious tenets of Methodism intact, they never quite shrugged off the Methodist mentality, which in their cases was a rather aseptic, unemotional piety—a stressing of low-key conservatism and self-containment that was only reinforced by the kindred aura of the Midwest. Although Johnny properly maintains all his family ties, they are not overtly affectionate ones; he is always just slightly cool and aloof. He is a dutiful son, however, and he recently moved his parents from Nebraska and set them up in semi-retirement in a pleasant part of Arizona.

Fade to Black

> I remember when I started this show, I was a young man with a dream. Now I'm an old man with a dream.
>
> —JOHNNY CARSON

I once asked Joanna what sort of things bother Johnny. She said, "Oh, he's pretty normal in the worrying respect—you know, he frets about the mortgage on the house, things like that." That a man of Johnny's immense wealth would even *have* a mortgage on his house, let alone have worries over it, is a sort of perverse notion. I think Joanna's statement was made partly out of obeisance to Johnny's beloved "common man" image—but there is also a ring of truth in it in that Johnny has a long-standing reputation for being tight with money. He literally hates to spend it—another typical trait, as I see it, of the Midwestern spirit.

The claim that Johnny Carson doesn't worry about

much except his mortgage—and, of course, his tennis game—is obviously not the whole truth about the man. His character points to a thousand little fears in a whole symphony of different ways. This is a man, after all, who sleeps with his baby pillow—who, in fact, won't travel without it and carries it everywhere in his suitcase.

He worries about opening in Las Vegas after a layoff, and he worries about not being the best. He worries about "The Tonight Show" and when the best time is to leave it; he wonders when it will start to go down, and he along with it. He has a love/hate relationship with the show—he wants to get out, to quit at the top, to escape the weekly bondage—but he also knows what it has done and is doing for him, and there is no assurance of what's on the other side of the wall.

Joanna admitted to me that she did not look forward to the time when Johnny would quit the show —not only for how it might affect him, but for the fact that he would then be around home constantly. I asked her if she thought it an imminent possibility, and she said, "I think he wants to retire at the top, but I find it very difficult to believe that he could quit, the show being as much a part of his life as it is. He talks about it, but I don't really think he could face it—at least not now."

Johnny himself told me at the time I left the show that he intended to give it another 18 months to two years, and then he was going to turn it over to a younger guy and move on. But Johnny has been saying that—to me, to the public, and to himself— for a long, long time.

I once asked Joanna under other auspices to do an "interview" with me, imagining that Johnny was actually dead. The idea made her nervous, but it also captured her imagination, so she agreed. Perhaps it was unwise that she did, because Johnny was uncomfortable to discover that she could be so cavalier about the subject.

I remember asking her if Johnny was afraid of death. She said he wasn't. I then asked her if he had specified any kind of particular arrangements for his funeral. She startled me by saying, "Oh, yes! Definitely. It's all planned out." I raised my eyebrows and Joanna went on: "Actually, there won't be a funeral. Johnny is much too private a person for that kind of exhibitionism. First of all, even though it's against the law, he has requested that he be cremated and that his ashes be scattered over the Pacific Ocean. That's done all the time out here—you know, there's even a small charter airplane service that specializes in doing nothing else. Anyway, Johnny has also specified that there won't be a church service or memorial ceremony of any kind, which will upset his parents, I'm sure."

It began to dawn on me that Johnny had even planned out his death scene—choreographing it as though for a casual acquaintance, playing with various possible effects. I asked Joanna if it would be a situation similar to what Jack and Mary Benny went through, in which on the day Jack was dying, all his friends came by the house and paid him their last respects. Joanna was aghast. "Oh, no," she said, "not like that! Johnny has set aside a great deal of money to pay for a huge party at Chasen's restaurant. The party will be on the day his ashes are scattered, and I'm to invite everyone who knew him over to Chasen's to have as much good food and as many drinks as they like—you know, just to have a good time. He wants me to be able to receive people away from the house, in a happy atmosphere where they can come and go as they like, or not at all if they don't want to come." Joanna paused and surveyed me carefully before continuing. "You know what happened recently? We were sitting in Chasen's having dinner and looking at the prices on the menu. I said jokingly to

Johnny, 'Johnny, inflation seems to have really hit poor Chasen's. I think you're going to have to put some more money in your death-party fund.'

"He just sort of hesitated for a minute, nodded thoughtfully, and said, 'You know, you're right. I'd better take care of that tomorrow.' "